Crash Course in Serving Spanish-Speakers

Recent Titles in
Libraries Unlimited Crash Course Series

Crash Course in Serving Spanish-Speakers

Salvador Avila

Crash Course

A Member of the Greenwood Publishing Group

Westport, Connecticut • London

Library of Congress Cataloging-in-Publication Data

Avila, Salvador.
  Crash course in serving Spanish-speakers / Salvador Avila.
        p. cm. — (Crash course series)
  Includes bibliographical references and index.
  ISBN 978–1–59158–713–2 (alk. paper)
  1. Hispanic Americans and libraries. 2. Libraries—Special
collections—Hispanic Americans. 3. Library outreach programs—United
States. I. Title.
  Z711.92.H56A95 2008
  027.6'3—dc22   2008031233

British Library Cataloguing in Publication Data is available.

Library of Congress Catalog Card Number: 2008031233
ISBN: 978–1–59158–713–2

First published in 2008

Libraries Unlimited, 88 Post Road West, Westport, CT 06881
A Member of the Greenwood Publishing Group, Inc.
www.lu.com

Printed in the United States of America

The paper used in this book complies with the
Permanent Paper Standard issued by the National
Information Standards Organization (Z39.48–1984).

10 9 8 7 6 5 4 3 2 1

Special thanks to those individuals that helped me make this happen:
Dr. Reynaldo & Dra. Marta Ayala
Daniel L. Walters
Ángel & Marina Micaela del Carmen Ávila
Sonia Gonzáles
Barbara Ittner & Blanche Woolls
Familia Avila del Valle Imperial, CALIFAS

CONTENTS

PREFACE

For the purpose of this conversation, Spanish-speakers will be defined as first generation individuals who were born outside of the United States, who primarily speak Spanish, who are recent arrivals to the United States and who reside in predominantly Spanish-speaking communities. It has been the author's observation that libraries are having an arduous time reaching out to the entire Latino population, specifically Spanish-speakers. What makes this task so grueling is that 72 percent of Spanish-dominant Latinos are first generation.

It is important to make a distinction between first-, second-, and third-generation individuals of Latino origin as each group has its unique characteristics. Even though second and third generations are of Latino heritage, they have different needs, expectations, values, and beliefs. For example, would a professional second-generation bilingual person need Spanish-language computer classes? Probably not. Would a first-generation Spanish-dominant gardener be interested in attending a leadership conference? Probably not. Would a third-generation English-dominant engineer listen to Spanish music as a leisurely activity? Probably not. These are just a few of the many examples that characterize the differences between generations in the Latino community.

So when libraries throughout the country are trying to offer library services to Spanish-speakers by housing Spanish collections, offering Spanish or bilingual story time, translating their literature to Spanish, and employing Spanish-speaking staff, one is to believe that they are undertaking a concerted effort to appeal to this segment of the community. That is why this crash course will solely focus on adult first-generation Spanish-speakers and might slightly touch on second- or third-generation Latinos who might be bilingual in English and Spanish or be English-dominant.

So where exactly do Spanish-speakers come from? The chart below published by D. J. Case & Associates (See Table) shows the regions and countries of Spanish-speakers.

Even though Spanish is universal in these countries, each nation has its unique dialects, terms, and expressions. What does this mean for libraries? Well, if a library is located in an area with a large Colombian community, its staff might want to acquaint themselves with that community and become familiar with some of their intricacies. They may also want to consider the fact that the Spanish dialect spoken may vary from region to region in a single country.

Even with the many different types of idioms that are used in Spanish-speaking communities, librarians need to understand that language is the one key common factor in the Spanish-speaking community. Institutions such as libraries need to grasp the fact that providing services to Spanish-speakers is a great opportunity, but one with growing pains. Until recently these growing pains stemmed from the fact that the library industry has had to deal with this underserved population without much experience, and few library professionals have passionately served mainly Spanish-speakers. Now, Spanish-speakers are being noticed and receiving much more attention, obliging libraries and staff to address their needs. And since there are signs that the Spanish-speaking community will retain its language for years to come, libraries need to establish themselves as a trusted community source so that these individuals start and continue to use library services.

This book will underscore the importance of reaching out to Spanish-speakers utilizing Spanish-language approaches that, most importantly, relate to Spanish-speakers on a cultural level.

Spanish-Speaking Countries

| Region | North America | Latin America | | Caribbean | Europe | Africa |
		Central America	*South America*			
Country	Mexico	Costa Rica	Argentina	Cuba	Spain	Equatorial Guinea
		El Salvador	Bolivia	Dominican Republic		
		Guatemala	Chile	Puerto Rico		
		Honduras	Colombia			
		Nicaragua	Ecuador			
		Panama	Paraguay			
			Peru			
			Uruguay			
			Venezuela			

If libraries want to effectively connect with Latinos and Spanish-speakers, they must address their needs and wants from a cultural perspective. As businesses compete in the Spanish-language marketplace, they must be one step ahead of the competition. Libraries must also compete as a business with other entities that are addressing similar needs. Fortunately, libraries may thrive if they embrace the ideas offered in this crash course.

The significant growth of Latinos is well documented. Since we have established that we will be focusing on first-generation Spanish-speakers in this book, our first step will be to achieve an in-depth understanding of this community. We must understand who they are and who they are not. One of the first steps is knowing what terms Spanish-speakers use to describe themselves. For example, if you were to ask a first-generation Spanish-speaker what his/her ethnicity/race/nationality is, what do you think that they would say? Well, most first-generation Spanish-speakers would respond with their country of origin, and more specifically the state that they are from. A sample response is "*Yo soy de Michoacan,*" or "I am from Michoacan."

Another common dilemma is whether we should refer to the entire population as Latino or Hispanic. One of the best responses to this predicament comes from an article titled "Catering to the Hispanic Market," written by Gregg Wartgow and published in the *Yard & Garden Dealer Success Guide*, which states that "generally speaking the two terms can be used interchangeably. However, the term Hispanics is typically used when referring to this population as a segment of the marketplace, but when referring to a specific people and/or culture from a Latin American country, Latino is the more precise, sensitive term." Going back to the previous question on labels, if you were to ask a second- or third-generation individual what his or her ethnicity/race/nationality is, what would they say? More often than not, the response would be that he or she is a U.S. citizen who happens to be of Latino heritage.

This crash course discusses the evolution and myriad approaches aimed at Spanish-speakers. Conventional wisdom would say that you attract this segment by simply having Spanish collections, offering bilingual story time, and having bilingual staff. These are still core requirements, but as society evolves, so must the approaches. That said, enjoy your journey into providing enduring, relevant, and responsive library services to Spanish-speakers.

FURTHER READING

Crouch, Ned. *Mexicans & Americans: Cracking the Cultural Code.* Yarmouth, Maine: Intercultural Press, 2004.

FURTHER WATCHING

Mi Familia / My Family. Directed by Gregory Nava. DVD. New Line Home Video.

INTRODUCTION

¡Bienvenidos! Welcome to the world of providing relevant and responsive library services and programs to Spanish-speakers. This book will be a resourceful tool for those library systems wishing to offer library services to Spanish-speaking communities. *Crash Course in Serving Spanish-Speakers* has been developed to assist library staff in meeting the needs and demands of the emerging Spanish-speaking community and addresses opportunities that exist within this rapidly growing community.

This book presents the author's views, recommendations, and anecdotes about nontraditional approaches to serving Spanish-speakers. With today's ever-changing landscape, due in large part to the increase of diverse communities, libraries and librarians need to keep abreast of the most current trends and best practices for providing connecting and enduring library services. *Crash Course in Serving Spanish-Speakers* will help you in achieve this goal.

Providing library services to Spanish-speakers is much more than housing Spanish-language collections, offering bilingual story time, and employing Spanish-speaking staff. In this volume you will find information on several topics relating to library services for Spanish-speakers, including the latest cultural traits, behaviors, values, beliefs, experiences, strategies, non-library scientific research, stories, statistics, issues, Web sites, and program models, so that you and/or your library system may advocate and champion services to Spanish-speakers.

This book has been divided into chapters that present advice on how to truly resonate with Spanish-speakers by offering pragmatic and practical information. The "what," "who," "when," "where," "why," and "how" chapters are detailed accounts of things to consider for implementation and use when making library services available to Spanish-speakers. The chapters on outreach, services, programs, marketing, and Internet will highlight successful initiatives that are transferable to public libraries. Most chapters will have one or several recommended books or videos that elaborate more on the chapter's subject. One must consider that the Spanish-speaking community emerged a long time ago. In light of this significant growth, the library profession has been slow to respond to this societal transformation. This book will advance your presence within this community and afford you the luxury of creating public value in a community that has been able to succeed in an uneven playing field.

After reading this book you should know more about the principle and signature points of serving Spanish-speakers; have enhanced knowledge, understanding, and perceptions of this segment of the community; be able to translate community needs to library services; and be prepared to identify, address, and speak to the needs of Spanish-speaking communities.

CHAPTER 1

What Are Services to Spanish-Speakers?

This "what" chapter will highlight the many cultural characteristics that shape the Spanish-speaking community. Unlike any other underrepresented group in the United States, Spanish-speakers can no longer be attracted by language alone. The days are long gone when language by itself was the single determining factor when introducing and encouraging the use of any type of service—from private to public. Utilizing Spanish is still a good tool to employ, but organizations should start reframing and looking beyond language. This is what brings us to one of our first important lessons:

> *Se habla cultura*—we speak culture—is equally if not more important than
> *se habla Español*—we speak Spanish.

In a workshop environment, if participants were asked to close their eyes and shout the first thing that came to their mind when the keywords "Spanish-speakers" were mentioned, the responses could be "family," "food," "landscapers," "hardworking," "Mexico," "immigrants," "caring," "Catholic," and so on. Some might have a hard time determining one word to shout. This exercise not only highlights the diversity of this segment of the population but also tells much about library staff perception. We all see things differently because we all see things from a different lens and have varying experiences and knowledge about Spanish-speakers.

It is important to understand the similarities and differences between Spanish-speakers because we cannot value them if we do not know what they are. In all honesty, what do many of us know about the Spanish-speaking community besides the frequently broadcasted bad news that has alarmed many citizens? An extensive, ever-increasing body of research tells us that businesses, organizations, and libraries need to have some cultural dexterity.

The current and future library needs of Spanish-speakers are not that different from those of the general population. Services will need to incorporate more of an emphasis on knowledge, ideas, information exchange, and relationships, but, when dealing with Spanish-speakers, they will need to be coupled with a twist of cultural cleverness. Even when libraries try to forecast the needs of Spanish-speakers, their initiatives often fall short of success. This may be attributed to two factors. Factor one is that members of the Spanish-speaking community are in a transitory state of being. First, they arrive in the United States and find themselves a place to live where they may survive. After acclimating, they move on to a better part of town, and the cycle of upward mobility continues for a long period of time. The second factor is that the librarians' lack of research and understanding places their initiatives at risk.

What are services to Spanish-speakers? Because this is a changing population, it may be necessary to stop doing things the way they were done in the past, even if these practices served libraries well, and look at potential new approaches. A big portion of my belief on what services to Spanish-speakers are rests on the notion that library staff need to be aware of the cultural characteristics of this promising population. Librarians need to understand that in addition to being in the library business, libraries are in the community and people business. That means that staff members need to study and gain knowledge of Spanish-speakers just as much as they have studied English-language library services. For an example of this, see Beth Dempsey's article "Latinas in Need," which appeared in the November 15, 2007, edition of *Library Journal.* A lack of awareness of the cultural characteristics of Spanish-speakers means the difference between a positive and relevant relationship and a negative and nonrelevant relationship. This might mean breaking away from traditional, antiquated approaches that might run contrary to what most librarians have been taught.

Currently, libraries are well positioned to assist Spanish-speakers because there is no one else providing these types of services. Besides schools, there is probably no other social agency that is as instrumental in literacy and valuing the importance of books. However, in order to capitalize on this opportunity, there must be well-devised approaches. This is the challenge that most libraries face. The key to success, according to many marketing to Spanish-speaking books, is reaching the emotional core of the consumer.

In the library profession, this might mean that Spanish-speakers prefer actual advice rather than a referral. This is truly a revolutionary concept as librarians were taught to point to the reference book and not share personal insights. But there is a difference between sharing personal beliefs and giving advice. If a Spanish-speaker is seeking tax advice, naturally, the librarian should refer them to the right agency or area in the library. If the same Spanish-speaker is seeking college advice, the library staff motives, needs and wants behind those characteristics do influence you." That is why, when working with Spanish-speaking communities, it is important that you consider the following "do's" and "don'ts":

Do:

Be positive and proactive with Spanish-speakers
Adore and praise them legitimately
Touch them physically
Accept their playful teasing
Remember that they are more sensitive than they appear
Value their social interaction skills and personal connections
Remember they hold feelings deeply
Promote creative and fun activities for and with them
Enjoy their charismatic innocence
Allow them opportunities for verbal expression

Don't:

Be too serious or sober in criticism
Push them too intensely
Ignore them
Forget they have "down" time also
Demand perfection
Expect them to dwell on problems
Give them too much rope (or they may metaphorically hang themselves!)
Classify them as just lightweight social butterflies
Attack their sensitivity or be unforgiving
Totally control their schedules or consume their time

Once you understand the complexities of the cultural characteristics of Spanish-speakers, and your library system has decided to use this cultural awareness in your transactions with Spanish-speakers, you will need to consider the following five aspects, which are instrumental in being successful and demonstrating commitment:

1. Justify entry into Spanish-speaking community. Are the services you offer appropriate to the community's needs?
2. Ensure that there is management and internal support. A good way of achieving support is to include cultural awareness competency, services, and programs.
3. Attend cultural awareness/diversity/inclusion training. A conference by the Society of Human Resources Management on diversity might have more resident experts on serving Spanish-speakers than a library conference. In New Jersey, Peggy Cadigan organized a conference titled "One Community: Diversity in Libraries Conference," which centered on diversity issues in libraries.

4. Develop metrics and goals to succeed. For every goal or objective to start something, have a goal or objective of something to cease. This usually comes in the form of a strategic plan, as what gets measured gets done.
5. Build long-term relationships with the Spanish-speaking community. This is usually a three-year undertaking that necessitates constant involvement.

From the outset, the "what" chapter should give the reader a better understanding of the multifaceted Spanish-speaking community. Library systems and librarians alike should not be daunted by these complexities. The following chapters will capitalize on the usage of these cultural traits and translate them into the implementation and interconnection of superior library services.

Successful library services for Spanish-speakers are given by people with at least some awareness and understanding of the community. If you are new to serving Spanish-speakers, there are a few professional development opportunities that you may capitalize on that will bring you up to speed. Some of these opportunities are listed below.

BOOK EXPO AMERICA

Book Expo America (BEA) is a conference that characterizes itself as a librarian-friendly event. Some of the benefits of BEA are that they dedicate a section of their conference and programs to connecting librarians with publishers. Helpful for librarians is that some vendors use librarian-friendly floor decals and flashing buttons to catch the attention of prospective purchasers. Of particular importance are the Association of American Publishers (AAP) Publishing Latino Voices workshops that take place during the event. During these seminars, event-goers are exposed to a variety of Spanish-language book industry leaders, who share their thoughts on the best tactics to reach Hispanic readers. Two workshops that took place during the 2007 conference that librarians learned much from were "Celebrate the Best in Latina Literature 2007," and "Creating a Community of Hispanic Readers." For more information about BEA, visit their Web site at http://www.bookexpoamerica.com.

GUADALAJARA INTERNATIONAL BOOK FAIR

The Guadalajara International Book Fair, or Feria Internacional del Libro, is the most important exhibit of Spanish language books in the world. It is a place where authors, literary agents, librarians, booksellers, and more than 1,600 publishing houses from 39 countries congregate to exhibit, purchase, network, attend lectures and literary programs, and become familiar with the Spanish book publishing industry. One benefit of attending this book fair is that if you are a member of the American Library Association (ALA), you may apply for the American Library Association / Feria Internacional de Libro (ALA/FIL) Free Pass Program. What this entitles you to is three nights at the Plaza del Sol Hotel, three continental breakfasts, courtesy registration and $100 toward the cost of airfare, courtesy of ALA. Free passes are only awarded to 150 librarians who are interested in the area of Spanish language acquisition or are working to develop a Spanish language collection. For more information about the Guadalajara International Book Fair, visit http://www.ala.org/ala/iro/iroactivities/guadalajarabook.htm.

REFORMA

REFORMA, the National Association to Promote Library Services to Latinos and the Spanish Speaking, was founded in 1971 and is considered the premier organization catering to Spanish-speakers and Latinos. REFORMA has a listserv where members may ask questions and receive responses from librarians throughout the country. It offers programs in many states as well as national conferences on how to best serve this segment of the community. Many of its members have served Latinos and Spanish-speakers in many capacities and are more than happy to share their expertise. The organization is considered a clearinghouse of ideas, information, knowledge, and best practices. REFORMA has created a "Librarian's Toolkit for Responding Effectively to Anti-Immigrant Sentiment," which may be found on its Web site (www.reforma.org). This six-page document is designed as a starting point to help those who find themselves in a debate over the complex issue of immigration.

Frequently, the wrong question is posed: Why don't Spanish-speakers utilize our library services and programs? What we should be asking is why aren't libraries doing a better job of introducing and encouraging the use of library services to Spanish-speakers? Often library staff express the sentiment since Spanish-speakers do not use the library's services, they should not be specially catered to. Those who ask these questions display low expectations and are not up to the challenge of rendering services.

"What" in essence is what needs to be carried out. What is even more important than "what" is "who" is going to ensure that the duties and responsibilities of serving Spanish-speakers are actually performed. There is a need to increase the number of library staff and public sector institutions interested in serving Spanish-speakers. Since much needs to be done in a short period of time, it is imperative that the library profession hire and train with the right outcome in mind.

What is the foundation that defines the right outcomes? For the most part, these are traditional services that librarians are familiar with. If these services are going to truly create public value, librarians need to have "what" in mind, but more importantly, they need to have the right "who." In the following chapter, we will review who makes a successful "who."

CHAPTER 2

Who Is Obligated to Provide Services to Spanish-Speakers?

This chapter discusses the matter of who should provide library services to Spanish-speakers. Libraries that will be successful in reaching out are those with an eye for emerging opportunities and who can then use their staff's competencies, skills, and talent in alignment with the needs of their customers and with the services the library provides. That is why it is central that library systems create opportunities where they exist, and not simply where they have been historically. This may be even more critical and more of a challenge in smaller communities where some of these solutions are more difficult to implement. Suggestions for overcoming this challenge include the following:

1. Hiring a librarian who is knowledgeable about social services. This might mean creating an outreach librarian position that will be tasked with introducing and encouraging the use of libraries in a nonlibrary setting. The best way to recruit librarians is to produce your own. Many librarians expect other people to do the work of motivating, recruiting, and ensuring that they attend and complete graduate school—hardly ever taking any vested interest. Now that libraries are seeing either a shortage of librarians and/or shortage of the right librarians, library boards are scrambling to fill these jobs. If

9

each librarian made it a point to motivate, recruit, and ensure that they were responsible for the accrual of just one more librarian, the profession would be in much better shape.

2. If staffing is an issue, one solution would be to reallocate current positions. This will be met with some resistance as many tenured librarians are good at what they have been doing for many years and fear stepping out of their comfort zone. Reallocating a reference librarian for an outreach position might be more necessary for your organization. Someone more like a social worker might be better suited for your library, as opposed to someone who simply likes to read.

3. Seeking volunteers who represent the Spanish-speaking community is ideal. One of the easiest ways to enlist assistance is to study who visits the library regularly with their family. It might be the mom who regularly attends all the children's programs, sitting in the back. However, be cautious in your approach when seeking volunteers. Slowly introduce the concept. Engage at a slow pace. Mentor them and watch the relationship mature.

4. Seek partnership opportunities with cultural groups. If you reside in a small town, finding this segment of the community is simple. A cultural characteristic of Spanish-speakers is that they enjoy celebrating their cultural heritage. If they know that you are there to advance their heritage, they will be receptive to your ideas.

This brings us to another important lesson:

Treating people equally does not mean treating them all the same.

The discussion of who should provide library services to Spanish-speakers raises many questions and perspectives. One may contemplate whether it should be a professional in the library business or a non-professional, and whether it should be someone from that cultural group versus someone not from that cultural group. According to Martin Gomez, author of "Who Is Most Qualified to Serve Our Ethnic-Minority Communities?" you do not have to be a librarian to offer library services and you do not have to be a member of that community, although these services are "in fact most effective when provided by librarians who are part of that cultural group that is being served."

Another way to approach this issue is to look at Spanish-speakers' perception of leadership. A few years ago the National Center for Latino Leadership produced a report titled "Reflecting an American Vista: The Character and Impact of Latino Leadership." The report highlighted the qualities Latinos want to see in leaders, organized into four traits that center on character, competence, compassion, and community service.

Character ideals that they wanted to see were leaders who keep their word and deliver on their promises by being good people who are honest and possess integrity. The Spanish-speaking community has heard too many times that librarians, or for that matter, many members from both the public and private sector, are interested in serving them. In seeking these services, the Spanish-speaking community has often discovered that there was a catch and/or that the individuals seeking their attention misrepresented themselves. Since the Spanish-speaking community knows that they are vulnerable due to their lack of English and/or lack of knowledge of the way business is conducted, they have a propensity to be victims. These people often know first hand what it means to live in a country where character is hard to find, so their expectations are somewhat higher when they come to the United States. It is important that librarians walk the walk and talk the talk.

The essence of competence is to be intelligent, experienced, and wise while producing results. The Spanish-speaking community has come to rely on the advice of professionals. In the United States it is their understanding that professionals such as teachers, lawyers, doctors and, yes, librarians hold respectable positions because of their knowledge of their disciplines. When a Spanish-speaker sees a Latino librarian they will open up faster than when dealing with a non-Latino librarian, as they perceive that the Latino librarian knows what it means to be an immigrant or the son/daughter of immigrants. Therefore, the interactions and conversations will be from an experienced, sound source.

Compassion contends that the kindhearted leader be humble, sincere, and sensitive. Spanish-speakers have experienced and witnessed corruption, traitors, and dishonesty. Their reluctance to trust is based on their experience with elected officials or supposedly important people from their native country, who said that they were acting in the people's best interests but whose actions proved otherwise. This leadership skill—compassion—forces librarians to be straightforward yet insightful into the needs of their patrons. An example of this skill at work could be in a conversation with Spanish-speakers about college. You might mention that, as parents, we know how important it is to send our children to college. While it might be desirable to have them stay home as a form of support, there are colleges in other states where our children can get a good education. Tell them to seriously consider this option as their children will be focused on their studies and will return as professionals. Then give them a list of universities that have proven track records educating Latinos.

The principle of community leadership is dedication and willingness to serve the community and help the community achieve its best possible way of life. If leaders are true community servants, they need to be in the public eye performing and offering good community activities. The Spanish-speaking community particularly likes to see individuals who they trust, such as librarians, rallying behind the Spanish-speaking community. Once you have earned their trust, outreach is the next part of the job.

For the most part, librarians have a good sense of how some societies function. Librarians usually take what they know for granted and they think this is the same for Spanish-speakers. For example, one might ask why Spanish-speakers and/or second-generation Latinos do not register to vote. Well, there are many reasons, but one should not assume that they know that they need to register in the first place. This is where a librarian can be of assistance. Librarians assigned to serving Spanish-speakers have a big responsibility. In addition to being familiar with in-depth demographic analysis, and the many diverse cultural characteristics, they must use these to figure out which library programs and services work and which don't work. It is important that the librarian assigned to Spanish-speakers be available as often as possible and stay abreast of the library's operations.

If you want to learn more about a candidate running for office, you can learn much by asking what services he or she would introduce to Spanish-speaking communities. The candidate's response will reveal whether they have an understanding of this community that they say they want to serve. Librarians in Spanish-speaking communities might be considered community servants and leaders who need to know how Latino societal issues work. This is why it is important to have the right staff serving this segment of the community. When the right librarian asks the right questions, community members have a true sense of the intent and impact of the question. If the wrong questions are asked, the community member will get the wrong impression, leading them to give misleading responses and ask the wrong questions themselves. One example of a wrong question is "Do you feel that reading is important?" The obvious answer would, of course, be a reassuring "Yes." A more appropriate question would be "What is important to you, and how may the library assist you?"

Some library professionals are miscast in their job, especially if they join the profession because they like to read and not because they want to help people. These people are more of a liability than an asset. The example given above, of asking questions that would elicit only a "Yes" answer, is characteristic of people who are not culturally sensitive. These questions elicit answers that are deceiving and misleading, and it is important not to fall into this trap. The "Yes" response leads the librarian to believe that they are on the same wavelength as the community member. The librarian presumes that because the community member agrees with the librarian that they may move on. What is actually happening is that the community member is agreeing out of respect to who they regard as a trustworthy librarian and avoiding being confrontational.

Table 1.3 in the previous chapter showed us that Spanish-speakers are not confrontational. They will not critique or directly pass judgment on library staff, or on anyone in a reputable position. What will happen is that they will become discouraged and stop using library services. In this chapter, the "who," which might be you, a peer, or someone to whom you report, needs to be current on literature that will raise concerns for and awareness of the Spanish-speaking community. For example, a recent finding by a two-year study titled "Multiple Origins, Uncertain Destinies—Hispanics and the American Future" found that "parents of Hispanic preschoolers are less likely than black, white and Asian parents to be fluent in English and less likely to read books to their children." The same study found that "participation in home literacy activities such as telling stories or visiting libraries is especially low for children reared in Spanish dominant homes." These findings ought to motivate most librarians to take action to promote reading among Spanish-speakers with children.

Managers who hire staff to work with the Spanish-speaking community need to select carefully. They need to determine the strengths of each potential hire and how these strengths would help to better serve the Spanish-speaking community. By being held accountable for the task of fulfilling their goals and objectives, the right hire will form healthy relationships with the community. A staff member with a sense of humor is also good, as humor helps interactions feel more genuine and is engaging for the patron. A sense of humor is especially appreciated by the Spanish-speaking community. The Spanish prank show *Ya Cayo* is a widely broadcasted hit. Another great example of Spanish humor for English-dominant or bilingual people is George Lopez. I highly recommend his comedy, as he discusses real Latino life with a comic twist.

Coaching librarians about the beliefs of Spanish-speakers is of the utmost importance as these beliefs relate to cultural convictions and ideals. Staff should be able to recognize these cultural details, be self assured, and not driven by monetary gain. Commending staff for a job well done will motivate them to continue doing what they do best: providing Spanish-speakers with the best customer service.

The following chapter looks at "when" to provide library services to Spanish-speakers. It will discuss some proven situations when is essential to make Spanish-language services available. It will also highlight holidays and approaches that resonate with Spanish-speakers.

FURTHER READING

Nevaer, Louis E. V. 2007. *HR and the New Hispanic Workforce: A Comprehensive Guide to Cultivating and Leveraging Employee Success.* Mountain View, Calif.: Davies-Black Publishing.

Santiago-Rivera, Azara L. 2002. *Counseling Latinos and La Familia: A Practical Guide.* Thousand Oaks, Calif.: Sage Publications.

Tienda, Marta. 2006. *Multiple Origins, Uncertain Destinies: Hispanics and the American Future: Panel on Hispanics in the United States.* Washington, D.C.: National Academies Press, 82.

CHAPTER 3

When Should You Provide Services to Spanish-Speakers?

This chapter offers a compelling case of and recommendations on when libraries should provide services to Spanish-speakers. In this situation, there are two options; either you take ACTion or you reACT. Because of the low expectations and predictability of library usage by Spanish-speakers and the large impact that this group can bring to our profession, we often feel perplexed and at a complete loss as to how to serve them. This brings us to one of the many points to consider when providing services to Spanish-speakers. Spanish-speakers are predictably unpredictable. This primary cultural characteristic of Spanish-speakers may result in a clash with the American way of doing business. Time and punctuality, for instance, are traits that are seen differently by those from Spanish-speaking cultures.

TIME

The Spanish-speaking community has a different perspective on time. This particular cultural characteristic might work for them in their native country, but it might be considered a detriment in the United States. To many native Spanish-speakers, time is not the single most important factor in determining the day's agenda or how much time they should spend doing a particular chore. This impacts their program attendance at libraries.

I once had a book discussion group that met every two weeks. The program was scheduled to take place at 2 P.M. in a central library location. The majority of the participants were females and a straw vote indicated that the day, location, and time were ideal. When the first day of the discussion group came, no one showed up. I waited patiently for about 20 minutes and still no one came. I picked up my things, turned off the lights, and locked the door. Just as I started walking to the service desk to resume my duties of staffing the desk, I noticed the group come in. They said that they were ready to start the book discussion group. I told them that we were to start at 2 P.M. The group replied that they were busy taking care of family affairs and got to the library as soon as they could. This continued to happen for the first several meetings. When I realized that the group was going to arrive late most of the time, I altered my schedule to reflect their outlook on time.

You may have heard Latinos use the term "Latino time." They are referring to the tendency of Latinos to begin an event late or arrive late to a particular function. This flexible perception of time is a widespread phenomenon in Spanish-speaking countries. Why is time a big issue? Because it is so deeply rooted in the way people do things.

PUNCTUALITY

To get a better understanding of Latino views on punctuality, I recommend an article written by Rick Vecchio titled "On Their Own Time: In Peru, Punctuality Is a Myth," featured in the July/August 2007 edition of *Psychology Today*. The president of Peru, Alan García, even asked his fellow citizens to synchronize their watches in a nationally televised ceremony, as his compatriots were known for being late. Being aware of this cultural characteristic is very important when serving Spanish-speakers as it is very relevant to things like program scheduling.

Pedro Rodriguez from the Portland Mexican consulate shares three elements that contribute to this time issue. First, people in Latin American countries feel that they may make up time anytime throughout the course of the day; therefore they are not necessarily tied to a schedule. It is not unusual for employees to arrive late to work. What ends up happening is that they make up the time at the end of the day. Secondly, since public transportation is much more common in urban cities in Latin American countries than in the United States, employees follow transportation schedules less rigidly. Lastly, many professions and/or occupations are salaried and not hourly; therefore, as long as the worker completes the task, everything is fine.

YEAR-ROUND SERVICE

Starting a strategic initiative to serve Spanish-speakers entails serving them year-round and not just when there are observances for Cinco de Mayo, Día de los Niños, or National Hispanic Heritage Month. Having services only on these holidays creates the perception that you are only an educational tourist, serving them only periodically. One of these events, however, does have particular significance, and this is National Hispanic Heritage Month. National Hispanic Heritage Month is one of the best times to celebrate, observe, and pay tribute to the many contributions that Latinos and Spanish-speakers have made to this country, but it is not the only time to render service. The following is a small historical note on National Hispanic Heritage Month.

President Lyndon B. Johnson started National Hispanic Heritage Week in 1968 to honor and acknowledge the presence of Latinos and Spanish-speakers in the United States. In 1988, President Ronald Regan extended the celebration to one month, which became National Hispanic Heritage Month. Since then, National Hispanic Heritage Month has been observed by the general population and especially by the Latino and Spanish-speaking community. Every year the president of the United States offers a proclamation in the name of National Hispanic Heritage Month. If you are new to serving Spanish-speakers, a simple Google search will supply you with an endless list of what different organizations, associations, and libraries are doing to celebrate this month, which takes place every year from September 15 through October 15. The number of Spanish-speaking Latinos in the United States continues to increase. Some of the most recent statistics state that by the year 2050, the U.S. Latino population will exceed 100 million—approximately 25 percent of the U.S. population.

Even though you should not be attached to a particular date or month and should provide services as they surface, there are many ways to go about establishing services and programs for Spanish-speakers. Capitalize on the opportunity to offer something worthwhile that will create public value in a responsive and relevant manner. The following are but a few examples of prime opportunities to reach out to Spanish-speakers.

RUBEN SALAZAR STAMP

In April 2008, the United States Postal Service (USPS) issued the "American Journalists" series of stamps. Only a handful of stamps featuring people are produced every year. With a careful screening process in place, only a few are selected to have their legacy on a USPS stamp. What is significant here is that in the set of five, a very prominent Latino is included—Ruben Salazar. Often Latinos and Spanish-speakers have been the afterthought of those making such decisions. But things like the Salazar stamp show that Latinos and Spanish-speakers are becoming more prominent than ever, and perhaps in the future, every day might be a day to highlight the achievements of Latinos.

When the Ruben Salazar stamp started circulating, librarians could have created a stamp display featuring prominent Latinos and Spanish-speakers. In June 1998, the USPS published a brochure titled *Hispanic People and Events on United States Postage Stamps*. This brochure features stamps honoring the Panama Canal, Puerto Rican elections, the Alamo, and Padre Junípero Serra, to name a few. Since the release of a stamp is not often tied specifically to any Latino holiday or event, it presents good opportunity to host a service or program at any time.

NEW BOOKS

Ever since it was revealed that Latinos were the largest underrepresented group in the United States, the book publishing industry has expanded production with many Latino-themed and Spanish-language publications. The release of a new publication presents a good opportunity for a library event. Purchase multiple copies of the publication and create a display featuring it and its genre. This resembles the "one book— one community" approach. Supplement it with other resources that will be of interest to the Latino population. The following examples are for English-language books, but you will see the pattern of what I am trying to relay to you as you can easily transfer this example to Spanish-language books. Benjamin Alire Sáenz published a book in 2008 titled *Names on a Map: A Novel*. It is the story of an individual who skips the U.S. draft and escapes to Mexico. A display of this book could be outfitted with other books with similar subject matter. Two new books you could display are *Not Anything* by Carmen Rodrigues and *Tales from the Town of Widows* by James Cañón. New books are a good draw as your library constituents are interested in reading the latest in literature. When a new book comes out, Latinos and Spanish-speakers will give it some serious consideration and are likely to check it out.

USING THE WORD "SPECIAL"

Now that we've focused on things to do, I'd like to discuss one thing we should stop doing—and that is to stop using the word "special." Too many times in the library world, when there is something new or something that librarians feel is unique, the word "special" is used. This should not be the case with Spanish-speakers. There should not be anything special about offering them a service or program. What makes that service or program special? Hispanic and Spanish-speakers are now the largest underrepresented group in the country, surpassing African Americans, and numbering in excess of 44.3 million. Library services are a piece of the pie that rightfully belongs to them. They might be special to the library as an organization, but that feeling should not be imposed on Spanish-speakers. When you are promoting or advocating library services to Spanish-speakers, avoiding words such as "special" is a good rule of thumb.

Providing successful services to Spanish-speakers takes time. One thing that I have learned throughout my years of extensive association with this community is that it can take several years of constant involvement to be seriously noticed. As stated previously, you must build your involvement in the community by joining organizations and participating in as many community events and committees as possible. Once started, programming must continue with regular events. Serving Spanish-speakers only at your convenience will seem half-hearted to the community. The message you want to send is that you understand the similarities and differences between your cultures, that you understand their family values, that you know their children's needs, and that you understand what makes them tick. Be ready to serve Spanish-speakers immediately and always.

One of the first things you need to do to successfully introduce and encourage the use of libraries is to learn what the people of the Spanish-speaking community know and what they don't know about the library. Be informed instead of making assumptions. For the most part, it has been my observation that librarians think Spanish-speakers don't know anything about libraries. They believe that Spanish-speakers come from countries that don't have library services. But this could not be farther from the truth. Many individuals, especially those who resided in urban areas in their home countries, are familiar with what a library is and what its services are. When they arrive in the United States, the only confusing part is the terminology between the two words—library and *biblioteca*. You will need to recap, share, introduce, and encourage the use of the library's services, but Spanish-speakers know what libraries are and how they can use them. For those Spanish-speakers that come from rural areas, the situation might be different. They might very well not be familiar with social services of any sort, including libraries.

Another misconception is that Spanish-speakers do not read. This is also not the case. Spanish-speakers are and have always been avid readers. What happens in many Spanish-speaking countries is that education is free up to a certain grade. After that point, education becomes less frequent. Graphic novels in particular have always been phenomenally popular in Spanish-speaking countries. Only recently have graphic novels been included in libraries here in the United States. We are witnessing the expansion of graphic novel collections and even conferences. Librarians are capitalizing on that reading experience. One of the most popular Mexican characters is Condorito. Condorito is a personification of a funny condor living in a fictitious town. The setting is typical of many small Chilean provincial towns and Condorito is meant to be a representation of the Chilean people.

There are several reasons why many librarians have not already embarked on serving Spanish-speakers. One of those concerns is False Evidence Appearing Real

(FEAR). The library profession has to contemplate that the culture it serves is changing faster than the culture it is used to, especially when it comes to serving diverse communities. Your attempts at providing services for Spanish-speakers may not initially be successful; you may need to try several different methods before you find one that works for your community. The Spanish-speaking community is a hard target to center on as its people are constantly on the move, especially in cities with growing Latino populations. As you are in a lifelong learning business, your efforts should never come to a complete stop. This is why constant involvement is essential.

Being available and making your presence known at cultural and social events throughout the year means you will always be there to answer questions. This will confirm your importance in the community. Most cities have some sort of Latino association, club, or chamber of commerce. Becoming involved with these organizations is a must, not just for the simple fact that you are supporting their endeavor, but because you will make yourself known and be remembered.

Allow me to share my own experience with the Las Vegas Latin Chamber of Commerce in Las Vegas, Nevada. The Las Vegas Chamber of Commerce offers several membership packages. For example, they have an individual membership that costs $200 and an associate membership that costs $175. The fee is slightly higher than an annual membership to the American Library Association and possibly your state library association. If you look at the return on your investment, you might find that a membership with your local Latino chamber of commerce is profitable. A well-organized association has monthly events that are good for networking and meeting other members from the business and nonprofit community. The benefit to joining such associations is that you have the opportunity to become an advocate for Latinos and Spanish-speakers in general and an ambassador for libraries. What has happened in my case is that over the course of years of constant involvement, people have forgotten my name and refer to me as the "library person." I earned this respected title by always having the library interest first in mind, and the Las Vegas Latino community knew that. In 2003, the Las Vegas Chamber of Commerce bestowed upon me one of their most coveted awards—the Award of Distinction in Culture—for the Las Vegas Clark County Library District's outreach efforts.

Once you have been noticed by the community, its members will come to respect you, and they will refer individuals, groups, and businesses to you if they have any library needs (such as sponsoring an exhibit). Eventually you will be sent people who are in need of educational and recreational resources. These newcomers will be delighted to know that you have a regular program for them at your library.

CHAPTER 4

Where Should You Provide Services to Spanish-Speakers?

This chapter offers suggestions of where library services should be provided to Spanish-speakers. Since we are focusing on first-generation and predominantly Spanish-speaking Latinos in densely populated areas, we need to become familiar with the community within the community. Because Spanish-speakers are in a transitory state of being, librarians who might consider them as new prospects do not have the luxury of second or third opportunities to make a first impression. This means librarians will do well to meet them on their turf, on their own ground, and within their social networks.

The Spanish-speaking community thrives on social networks and word-of-mouth approaches. The spread of information socially, by word-of-mouth, has been proven to attract people to businesses and organizations. Spanish-speakers are known to rely on the suggestions of those in their peer group when making a decision, whether that be where to purchase a vehicle or whether they should visit the library. This phenomenon works well with this segment of the community for several reasons. For starters, Spanish-speaking neighborhoods are truly tight communities. People talk to their neighbors, and those neighbors talk to their friends.

Another significant reason for this is that some Spanish-speakers come from rural and isolated societies, and they are accustomed to a more closed and exclusive social network, mainly of individuals with the same background, values, and experiences. They prefer to stay within or near this community for their social and business interactions. People whose social and business interactions are conducted strictly in Spanish tend to be geographically isolated because they stay in their neighborhoods and away from other communities where people do not speak Spanish.

This self-imposed isolation leads to the thorny aspect of where you must provide library services to Spanish-speakers. Once you start to get involved with the community and once you have determined who is going to play a part in providing library services, the next logical step is to settle on where to start or where a presence is needed. The best solution is to go to where the people come together. The most efficient and effective way to attract attention to your services is to go to those places where there are already captive audiences.

There are many positive points to setting up library services for Spanish-speakers in this way. For instance, all of the organizing and marketing will be done for you. Begin by representing your services using the right staff members, literature, and promotional items. Below are some suggestions of places where you might want to start your efforts. They are general in scope. Joining in school fairs, family literacy nights, community and cultural events, parades, chambers of commerce, and health agencies are just a few of many opportunities that exist.

Educational and cultural fairs are a good way to make your presence known. For the most part, educational and cultural fairs are happy to offer the library a free booth. Highlight that you will show parents and children how libraries can supplement their education. As part of your booth, you should have general literature that speaks to all of the services, resources, tools, and programs available. Of course, you must also make sure that some if not most of the literature that you provide is in Spanish. Great promotional giveaways, like pencils, rulers, and candy, will encourage children and their parents to pay your booth a visit. These are opportunities that libraries should not miss, as they can lead to activities and partnerships that will last long after the fair has ended. Fairs are an opportunity to speak, depending on the event, to hundreds or more community members. They also provide an opportunity for you to open a serious dialogue with members of the community, as well as identify and partner with other community organizations. You might even identify some talent that you can showcase in your facility. Many things can happen, it is all depends on where you go.

There are many different places and organizations where Spanish-speakers congregate that will maximize your library undertaking, but each community is different. One obvious one is the church. Besides the fact that most Spanish-speakers are religious, there is the fact that many churches conduct Spanish-language mass at convenient times. Most Spanish-speakers are religious, which is made evident by the hierarchical structure of Latino culture. For the most part they are Catholic; however, many do not remain loyal to the Catholic Church. More and more Spanish-speakers are seeking different denominations. The reason is that they do not feel that the Catholic Church is doing an adequate job of motivating them. The Catholic Church often encourages Spanish-speakers to be happy with what they have, to treat others well, and to continue believing. The messages from other houses of worship often emphasize how to be successful, how to make goals to be the best individual, and how to gain financial empowerment.

Once you determine which house of worship you plan to be working with, it is important to establish a link with either the priest/minister or his administrative secretary. An easy approach would be to establish contact with someone who frequents both the library and church and ask for permission to post library literature. This person should champion library services and should help the library promote events, services, or programs for Spanish-speakers.

Most Spanish-speaking neighborhoods have their own grocery stores, which are more commonly known as *carnicerias*—meat stores. In these stores there are many products that are not commonly found in traditional grocery stores. For example, you may find cans of *menudo* in traditional stores, but rarely find the fresh tripe that makes up the *menudo*. These types of *carnicerias* are a clearinghouse for Spanish-speakers.

One way of finding out about events in your community is by paying attention to radio and television stations and newspapers that cater to the Spanish-speaking community. These media outlets are always looking for educational and cultural activities for their readership. Becoming familiar with them is very important. What is even more important is to know the staff of each entity personally. That way the next time the library wants to promote a service or program, you can contact them directly instead of having your press release or publicity efforts land on their stack of incoming faxes and mail.

In small towns there might not be media outlets that cater directly to Spanish-speakers. In that case, turn to the second-best thing—the English-language newspaper! The best place in the English-language newspaper to promote your library services is in the classifieds section. Spanish-speakers might not know how to read English, or even Spanish, but many do know basic words in English. They are also interested, like most of us, in great buys. This could be where you will be most successful at promoting your services and programs. If you put a Spanish ad in the English classifieds, it will catch their attention all the more. Still, this method is not guaranteed. I have heard from librarians across the country that their newspaper ads were not very successful. It may take some trial and error before your efforts prove fruitful.

Family literacy nights take place during the course of the school year and are a way for schools to connect with parents. If schools in your area have such events, make sure that you are a stakeholder. Be part of the school committee that organizes the event. This will provide you with the added benefit of increasing your network.

Community and cultural events aim to strengthen Latino culture among Latinos themselves as well as introduce it to the general population. These are great places to put your conversation hat on as these are the yet another place where Spanish-speaking cultural groups and representatives will assemble. This is a prime opportunity to establish contacts. Inquire about the next community/cultural event planned and how you can get on mailing list for such events.

Parades are great events to participate in, worth the time, energy, and effort, though they are a lot of work. The approach that you take during these parades is very important. I have observed that parades focusing on entertainment and book characters do best, even if reading or library services are never mentioned. The crowd will be in for a surprise to know that it was their local library that offered the best entertainment. For an idea on what a library's contribution to a parade can look like, check out an article titled "Cruz Control" in the December 2003 edition of *American Libraries*. The article highlights how staff members of the Las Vegas/Clark County Library District impersonated the "Queen of Salsa," Celia Cruz. They were a hit, to say the least!

Local Latino or Hispanic chambers of commerce are good for networking. If you are lucky enough to have any of these organizations in your area, use it. If you aren't, Latino business owners are bound to congregate somewhere, like a local restaurant to discuss matters of importance to their community and how to further their businesses.

When meeting with these organizations, many librarians want to learn more about the Spanish-speaking community. However, many, when speaking with the executive director or manager of such an organization ask the wrong questions such as, "What is the make-up of the Latino population in this city?" or, "How can the library be of assistance?" The librarian should be able to use his or her research skills to determine this information beforehand so that the actual needs of the community can be addressed in-depth. It is always positive for you to meet as many library supporters as you can find, but there are other members of the community who could be of greater assistance. This is especially true in big cities where there is a wealth of resources; however in a small town, you have no option but to meet the limited number of individuals and organizations.

In larger towns and cities, most social service providers, including libraries, have a liaison, representative, or staff member who works directly with Latinos or Spanish-speakers. Having such a position is the most cost effective method of making your presence known in the community, as this person will be able to establish a network with other such liaisons in other social services organizations. In a small library without such a position, you may be the person to find the individuals and organizations with which you can interact.

The above-mentioned organizations and events are involved throughout the course of the year in working with the Spanish-speaking community and drawing its people together. Joining forces with these organizations is probably the most cost-effective and efficient way to attract Spanish-speakers to the library. Housing Spanish-language collections, offering Spanish or bilingual story time, translating literature into Spanish, and employing Spanish-speaking staff is not enough, nor is it the most cost-effective use of your time.

Now that we know where to start introducing and encouraging the use of library services to Spanish-speakers, we need to dig deeper into why it is so necessary to serve this segment of the community. In today's world, where librarians are finding themselves competing with budget crises, for convenience factors, for technology, and with other organizations for the deliverance of high-quality services, librarians need to start justifying their existence. Every once in a while, studies surface that highlight the way libraries prevail in meeting the community's needs in general. But let's look to see if this is the case for Spanish-speakers. The following "why" chapter will talk about the sophistication that will be needed to provide synergy for the expansion of library services to Spanish-speakers.

CHAPTER 5

Why Should You Provide Services to Spanish-Speakers?

And the trouble is, if you don't risk anything, you risk even more.
—Erica Jong, *How to Save Your Own Life*

If Spanish-speakers make up a large percentage of your community's population, a better question might be a rhetorical one: why *not* provide services to Spanish-speakers? Libraries are there to serve everyone, including Spanish-speakers. This chapter discusses why it is important to provide library services to Spanish-speakers and create a community of Spanish-speaking readers.

After Mexico, the United States is the second-largest Spanish-speaking country in the world. Many organizations and institutions have reached a plateau with the general population and need to bank on the Spanish-speaking community for their next growth strategy. Where many businesses have seen their usage either stagnate or decline, opportunities exist with underserved and underrepresented communities.

Every section of our country is going to have an influx or segment of Spanish-speakers in their community. For example, in California and Texas, the number of Josés has become greater than the number of Johns. In Geraldo Rivera's new book (which I recommend), *Hispanic: Why Americans Fear Hispanics in the U.S.*, he writes: "While the name Smith still ranks as the most common surname in the United States,

27

for the first time, according to a survey released by the Census Bureau, two Hispanic surnames, Garcia and Rodriguez, are among the top ten. Another, Martinez, was narrowly edged out of tenth place by Wilson."

Why it is that businesses and organizations do not acknowledge the phenomenon of emerging diverse communities, in this case the Spanish-speakers, until they have become well established? This is mostly because it is easier to focus on the things we already know, and we fail to take into consideration that which we don't know. Services for Spanish-speakers can be very important for the library, but often this makes library staff uneasy. In many cases, you will find staff who resent serving this segment of the community. That is why during these times of demographic change, thinking about the future becomes more difficult—and more necessary.

During these times of transformation, librarians need to reframe their professional ideology. This might entail an overhaul of the way traditional services are offered, with technological or cultural alterations. Without making these compulsory changes, our profession becomes less relevant. Overcoming employees' resentment at having to serve Spanish-speakers is only the beginning. Cultural diversity training works best when there is a need for it and when the trainer understands both diversity and library issues and knows how the two are connected. Too many times a cultural diversity trainer or company consultant is brought in to educate librarians about the importance and impact of cultural diversity, but rarely does that training offer skills that are transferable or applicable to the library profession. Finding the right consultant or trainer should be a slow and cautious process. A successful consultant or trainer will help librarians admit and understand their biases about serving Spanish-speakers and make them aware of how their actions or inactions affect each transaction. The fact is, there are a good number of librarians who are silently yet adamantly against serving Spanish-speakers—and yes, they are likely to be at least a few in your own library.

The present escalating Spanish-speaking and second-generation Latino communities are making sure that the private and public sectors notice them and address their needs and wants. As members of the public sector, librarians must begin changing the way they cater to these communities. The Spanish-speaking community has many sources available for their own success and for their daily needs, and this does not automatically include your library. Many social services providers offer their daily necessities. That is why it is essential for you to become familiar with their cultural characteristics and take on the role of a school or university counselor, instead of simply that of librarian, when they enter your building.

The following questions are ones that warrant consideration:

- What do most librarians really know about the Spanish-speaking community?
- How do we really know that the services offered by libraries are reaching this community and/or creating public value?
- What do library services to Spanish-speakers look like?
- How successful are we at serving Spanish-speakers every day?
- Do we honestly believe that we are offering relevant and responsive library services to Spanish-speakers?

One recent success, according to an article titled "Economics of Outreach to Diverse Communities" in an Urban Libraries Council newsletter, is that "library outreach to new immigrants and multilingual–multinational communities can be viewed through the same economic development prism—in other words, our role as a gateway, especially where early literacy, workforce development and small business start-ups are concerned, contributes to the economic health of our communities."

Another success that highlights how Latinos and/or Spanish-speakers are part of mainstream America can be found in a November 2005 *Hispanic Magazine* article titled "Panorama Latinos," which states: "When it comes to iconic marketing fame, whose face is the most popular? Cap'n Crunch's? No. The Energizer Bunny's? Nope. Charlie the Tuna's? Tampoco. It's none other than the beloved and world famous coffee man Juan Valdez. The mustachioed Colombian beat out 25 other icons nominated for the Favorite Advertising Icon prize by Advertising Week. Valdez got a spot on Madison Avenue's Walk of Fame, along side last year's winner: the M&M characters."

Plenty of evidence underscores the impact that Spanish-speakers are having in their communities, and Latinos are becoming more and more successful. Some recent notable contributions of Latinos that highlight why it is important to serve Spanish-speakers include the following:

- Carlos Slim Helú is now the richest person on earth, bypassing Bill Gates
- William D. Perez has become the first nonfamily Chief Operating Officer and President of the Wrigley Jr. Company
- Miss Puerto Rico won the title of Miss Universe in 2008
- Dr. Elsa Murano became president of the sixth largest university, Texas A&M University

On a tragic note is the little-known story of Marine Lance Corporal José Gutierrez, a 28-year-old Guatemalan immigrant, who was the first U.S. soldier killed in Iraq. Lance Cpl. Gutierrez was awarded U.S. citizenship after he was killed. The list of notable Latinos goes on and on.

The Public Library Association, a division of the American Library Association, is advancing emerging services for Spanish-speakers. Some examples are: "Welcome to the U.S.: Services for New Immigrants," "Celebrate Diversity: Cultural Awareness," and "Know Your Community: Community Resources Spaces."

Under the "Welcome to the U.S.: Services for New Immigrants" program, libraries will have information on citizenship, English as a Second Language (ESL) courses, and a variety of other social services to help Latinos participate fully in U.S. society. Many libraries throughout the country offer ESL classes. A few are clearinghouses for citizenship information and provide citizenship classes to help Latinos gain citizenship status. Big cities have the luxury of having agencies or funding to sponsor these types of service priorities. If you find yourself in a smaller town with limited resources, the library may ultimately be the only organization to offer these workshops. Services such as these are arguably part of a librarian's duties and responsibilities. It is not difficult to offer such workshops. You might find a volunteer in the community who can assist you in providing this information for your clientele.

The program, "Celebrate Diversity: Cultural Awareness," observes and celebrates Latino cultural heritage. The purpose of this service priority is twofold. One is to pay tribute to the history, contributions, and impact of Spanish-speakers in our society. The second attribute is to expose this first purpose to the entire community. Popular celebrations include Cinco de Mayo, Día de los Muertos, Día de los Niños, and National Hispanic Heritage Month. One of the fastest ways to champion cultural awareness if you do not have the resources is to invite a member of the public to share with the library his/her cultural arts and crafts, souvenirs, and native possessions. These could be presented in the form of an exhibit.

The "Know Your Community: Community Resources Spaces" program encourages libraries to provide information about community agencies and their services. Libraries under this program aim to become clearinghouses of information for other organizations, associations, groups, societies, and entities that have goals similar to those of the library. A section of the library is dedicated to bulletins, literature, and brochures to inform people about other similar services in the community. If the most pressing needs of a community are transportation, translations, and ESL, a helpful library would have information about public transportation, agencies that offer translation services, if any, and a listing of all the locations in town or in the nearby community that offer ESL classes.

Another reason why we need to start and/or continue providing library services is to dispel the many myths about immigration as it relates to Spanish-speakers. Many of these myths are full of falsehood and stories that are fabricated to advance someone else's beliefs. In a September 2007 *DiversityInc* magazine article, author Yoji Cole takes a close look at ten myths about immigrants. One example from the article: "The claim: Most immigrants cross the border illegally. The facts: Around 75 percent of today's immigrants have legal, permanent visas, and of the 25 percent who are undocumented, 40 percent overstayed temporary visas."

Many Spanish-speakers, especially the ones of Mexican heritage who remain in the United States, are seen as a disappointment by their peers back home. It is fine for them to come on a temporary basis, but there is a common feeling that the United States is not their home and that they are expected to return home. While there are many successes, much work lies ahead. Young Spanish-speaking adults of Mexican heritage yearn for the basics, a job and security. The librarian's role is to facilitate their journey by highlighting options that will help them become more successful. They are not seeking a lecture or sermon about how reading is important. In past generations, many underrepresented groups assimilated to succeed. Nowadays, the Spanish-speaking community only needs to adapt to their new society to succeed and not necessarily assimilate. Many people are not comfortable with this fact. What these individuals need to realize is that over time, usually three generations, these underrepresented groups become fully integrated into society and assimilate by default.

Unfortunately, if you read the National Endowment for the Arts publication "Reading at Risk," it will share that "literary reading is declining among Hispanics," that the "lowest reading rate is among male Hispanic Americans," and that "there is no consistent pattern of library reading among Hispanic Americans." In order for libraries to be successful they need to facilitate the tenure of the Spanish-speaking community in the United States. The issue for organizations such as libraries is no longer why they should render these services, but how are they going to connect with this new Spanish-speaking population.

Librarians need to gain a painstaking understanding of all of the reason why they need to serve Spanish-speakers. They need to recognize that new markets entail new approaches. New trends entail new service and program creation. Traditionally, Spanish-speakers were found in metropolitan areas such as California, Texas, and New York, to name a few. In this new landscape, that you will find them in nontraditional nonmetropolitan areas. Anywhere there is an industry that needs cheap labor, Spanish-speakers will be there. Arkansas, Georgia, and Louisiana are but a few states that have experienced tremendous growth in the Spanish-speaking population.

Now that we have touched on "what," "who," "when," where," and "why" it is important to provide library services, we need to address the right approach—more importantly, "how" should you provide services to Spanish-speakers? The following chapter will reveal best practices with an emphasis on how to provide culturally relevant information that keeps up with the needs of today's Spanish-speaking community.

FURTHER READING

Rivera, Geraldo. 2008. *Hispanic: Why Americans Fear Hispanics in the U.S.* New York: Celebra.

CHAPTER 6

How Should You Provide Services to Spanish-Speakers?

This chapter provides information on best practices and how librarians need to reframe some or many of their approaches as we challenge conventional wisdom and look at the link between libraries and Spanish-speakers. It will discuss perceptions, translations, transcreations, and the notary public comparison. Translation is the process of rendering one language into another language. Transcreation is the process of forming a different message with the primary message in mind. We will discuss both of these in further detail later on in this chapter. But we must start with the psychological aspects to the situation of serving Spanish-speakers.

Psychologically, librarians need to understand that they will not see themselves in the Spanish-speaking patron. Once they understand this, they must see that a new methodology is essential. In this situation, understanding the cultural nuances of Spanish-speakers is more relevant than understanding the language itself. Hence we come to another important lesson: Find out what is Latino within your services and approach the Spanish-speaking community from that standpoint. The best way to understand and serve a certain type of patron is to try to be that patron, to walk a mile in your patron's shoes.

The public sector, especially librarians, should reject the idea of being like the private sector when it comes to reaching Spanish-speakers mainly because the private sector often is not employing culturally relevant messages. The examples from the private sector that I am employing in this Crash Course are ones from companies that have employed positive cultural approaches and messages. Many of these practices are, at best, good practices. However, librarians need to look at the current great practices within our library profession. A library should not be run like a private business.

Before we talk about the perceptions, translations, transcreations, and the notary public comparison, let's present a developmental scenario. Let's pretend that you have been charged with creating a new soft drink for the Spanish-speaking community. This beverage is to be created for, marketed to, and enjoyed by Spanish-speakers. There are no limitations to your drink conception. You may alter an already existing drink or start from scratch.

What would be some of the contributing factors to play a role in your development of such a soft drink? How would you go about researching Latino tastes? What would you consider when making such decisions? What else would you examine during your research? How long would the entire process take? Now ask yourself, does my library take all of these questions into account when delivering services to Spanish-speakers?

Here are some examples on how beverage companies are producing such soft drinks. They will consider if refrigerated juices, bottled water, carbonated, sport, and energy drinks are preferred. They will also learn that Latinos prefer a sweeter taste. People from the Caribbean tend to prefer nectars; those from Mexico prefer *aguas frescas*, berry, lemon, lime, and orange flavors. As for what serving size to sell, larger households would require bigger containers; but if there are several families within a household, smaller, individual drinks might work better. Some proven products are Kerns Horchata, Kool-Aid Tamarindo and Coca-Cola with Lime. Also, remember that your target consumer will also be consuming the same drinks as the general population; therefore, you will need a cultural message to earn their loyalty.

Now let's apply this sort of development scenario to library services. You are a small-town library, or a medium-to-large public library. Demographic research reveals that 15 percent of your population is of Latino heritage and that most of them primarily speak Spanish. Because most of them work in the poultry farms or local industry, we are assuming that they are, for the most part, not well educated and low-paid. From this demographic information, we gather that the Spanish-speakers are a vital part of your town's social, economic, and cultural landscape.

If you have no Spanish-speaking staff, collections, or services that meet the needs of Spanish-speakers, what should be your first step in introducing and encouraging the use of library services? Become familiar with many of the cultural characteristics and personality traits of Spanish-speakers, many of which are highlighted in depth in the first few chapters. In addition to being aware of these characteristics and traits, you must take them to heart. These should not be considered principles that you have picked up in a training session and hope to use one day, nor should they be stored like handouts in a filing cabinet. In order to be successful, you must honestly make serving Spanish-speakers one of the top priorities of your library.

You must also become familiar with your local constituents. You cannot afford to lump them into one category, whether that is Latino, Mexican, or Colombian. Once you have a better idea of the make-up of your local Latino population, start by seeing what other, if any, resources they are using. Since actions speak louder than words, observing their actions will indicate what they deem as important. The more research and data you have done before you begin contemplating what services you will offer, the better your services will be when it is actually time to implement them. These are baby steps that will take weeks, if not months, to complete. Do not let time discourage you from continuing to reach your Spanish-speaking community.

PERCEPTION

The perceptions and expectations of Spanish-speakers differ from that of the general U.S. population. Two characteristics of Spanish-speakers are that they are polymorphic and fatalistic. Polymorphic people tend to rely on other individuals for their existence and way of carrying out business. For example, Spanish-speakers often depend on professionals for additional advice in subject areas other than the professional's specialty. This is manifested in that Spanish-speakers are puzzled by that fact that they cannot go to a pharmacy and receive medication without a doctor's prescription. In their native countries, they would see a pharmacist for professional advice and counsel as well as the dispensing of medication. To Spanish-speakers, a pharmacist is a well-respected professional.

Some people think that Spanish-speakers are not familiar with library services in their native countries, so that when they arrive in the United States, they do not use such services or seek them out. This is not necessarily true. Many Spanish-speakers, depending on what country and region they are from, are familiar with library services in their native country. However, some do not know about library services. Once you are able to bring Spanish-speakers into the library, something unique happens. While you are trying to increase the circulation of your Spanish materials, your records might also reflect an increase in the popularity of other English-language materials. Spanish-speakers will take advantage of the Spanish collections, but they are also interested in popular English materials. Don't pigeonhole them as using strictly Spanish collections and resources. They know and understand that to be successful, they need to polish and practice their English, and one way of doing that is to borrow English-language materials.

Spanish-speakers are also tend to be fatalistic, meaning they don't believe that they have control of the future and therefore only focus on today's issues. This concept may reveal itself in the form of not using library services, as they are busy putting their families first, working physically demanding jobs, and often working more than multiple jobs that consume most of their time and energy.

TRANSLATION VS. TRANSCREATION

Translation is the process of rendering one language into another language. For the most part this means speech or text, usually in English, which is then to be translated into Spanish—a fairly straightforward activity. Translation works in many cases, but we need to be aware of the times when it might not work. Let's take a look at some library terminology that can be easily translated.

English	Spanish
self-check	*auto servicios* or *auto registro*
library	*biblioteca*
book discussion group	*club de lectores*

Now let's look at the word "circulation." If you were to translate this word into Spanish, the word would be *circulación*. But in a predominantly Spanish-speaking community, where the term does not carry a meaning associated with libraries, a sign that said *circulación* would make no sense. Instead it is more effective to use other terms that capture the spirit of the word. *Préstamo*, for instance, means to loan. Therefore, a sign with the word *préstamo* might make more sense. In many Spanish-speaking countries the word *salida*, meaning to exit, is used for their circulation function. One of the best-known marketers to Spanish-speaking communities, Felipe Korzenny, has said that "it is very difficult for a translation to do justice to the original for the reasons that the cultural elements in the original communication were not designed with the second culture in mind."

TRANSCREATION

According to Chrysanthe G. Sawyer in her article titled "Marketing to Hispanics Requires a Culture-Specific Approach," "transcreation is taking the essence of the current marketing message and expressing that essence with words, phrases and visuals that resonate best with the Hispanic culture." Transcreation involves looking at the text that needs to be converted from English to Spanish and rewording it in the new language while retaining the essence of its original meaning.

Listed below are some nonlibrary examples of how transcreation can best be used. All of the following English phrases are well-recognized ad slogans. Let's look at the slogan "An American Revolution," used by Chevrolet. If you were to translate the phrase you come up with *una revolución americana*, a completely nonrelevant phrase to Spanish-speakers. But if you employ the art of transcreation, you might use the word *súbete*, meaning to come on board. *Súbete* makes more sense than *una revolución americana* as the commercial or promotional piece would have other phrases to complement this word. In Mexico, Chevrolet uses the word *conócelo*, to become familiar with, as their choice for the catchy slogan. Chevrolet employs completely different approaches to their slogan depending on the country they are advertising to. Here are some other transcreated ad slogans:

English	**Spanish**
moving forward	*avanza confiado* (traveling confidently)
let's build something together	*juntos mejoramos su hogar* (together we better your home)
stick together	*estamos juntos* (we're together)

You need to be keenly aware of the meaning of your words when creating posters or flyers to attract Spanish-speakers. Always ask whether a phrase can adequately be translated or if it needs to be transcreated. Librarians also need to look at how they are approaching the Spanish-speaking community. The library rhetoric used will leave an impression that will either negatively or positively impact Spanish-speakers. The following are two types of approaches that illustrate how a message can best be adapted to speak to the Spanish-speaking community. The first example comes from the private industry, specifically a bank, while the second example comes from a library.

Old Approach

Low APR, free checking, automatic withdrawals from checking or savings account, etc.

New Approach

Our institution is interested in guiding you through the confusing process of fulfilling your dreams and taking care of your family's best interests. Our friendly and knowledgeable staff will guide you through the process so that you know exactly how your hard-earned money will be put to use.

Old Approach

Spanish collections, bilingual story time, Spanish-speaking staff.

New Approach

The library is a place where you may find books to help your children complete their homework assignments, as well as a place where you will be motivated to learn more about this country and how to succeed in it. Remember that you are here to succeed and the library is one of the many resources that will help you achieve your family's goal.

By now I hope you have noticed that being culturally sensitive and reframing your approach is of the utmost importance. As institutions such as libraries and librarians continue to pound away at earning their patronage, there are additional issues that we need to be aware of. For example, Spanish is one-third longer than English. So when you have a catchy English phrase, remember its the Spanish translation is likely to be longer. This is another reason why you should consider employing and becoming familiar with transcreation.

As an example of best practices, the following is a public sector flyer promoting an upcoming holiday program. Keep in mind that the flyer is missing holiday artwork such as ornamental balls, *piñatas*, candy, and sponsors' logos to catch people's attention. The main point of highlighting this poster is to review the terminology it uses. This poster incorporates all of the best practices we have discussed. Some parts have been translated; some have been transcreated; some have been left alone.

NOTARY PUBLIC

If you want to understand and appreciate the Spanish-speaking community, it would be prudent to know where they come from—not just geographically, but as related to their cultural paradigm. One prime example is to understand what the role of a librarian is and compare that role with a similar one in a Latino country. Here we will compare the job of a librarian with that of a notary public in a Spanish-speaking country, as in many way their roles are similar.

In most U.S. states the notary public is governed by the Secretary of State. The purpose of the notary public, as we know it, is to be the official witness to the signing of a document. They basically acknowledge that the signer is the person they claim to be, sign a notorial journal, and stamp the document. Then they are paid a fee and the transaction is complete. This is often the full extent of what a person working as a notary public does. Often being a notary public is a job had in addition to another position, such as a banker.

In many parts of the country where there is a large influx of Spanish-speakers, there are bound to be companies that will exploit this segment of the community. That is why some states have drafted laws requiring notaries rendering services in languages other than English in Spanish-speaking communities to post a sign declaring that they are not an attorney in the state, are not licensed to give legal advice, and may not accept fees for giving legal advice.

In Latin American countries, the notary public or *notario público* plays a slightly different role. A *notario público* is a respected profession filled only by educated individuals. They are turned to for legal advice and counseling and perform many important tasks similar to those of a notary in the United States. They also provide assistance in many matters and on varying subjects. They are respected and held in high regard for the sound guidance they provide, and they are paid accordingly.

ENGLISH FLYER

Beyond the Neon. Performing Arts Division • City of Las Vegas Department of
Leisure Services
The Las Vegas City Council invites you to join **Mayor Pro Tem Gary Reese** for
a December Fiesta!
Saturday, December 16, 2006, 5–8 P.M.
Come one, come all! Celebrate the season with a traditional Hispanic holiday
festival for the entire community.

- Caroling
- Santa Claus
- Live Entertainment
- Food Vendors

All ages welcome.

Free

Call 229-1515 for more information
East Las Vegas Community / Senior Center
250 N. Eastern Avenue
www.artslasvegas.org
www.lasvegasparksandrec.com

SPANISH FLYER

Beyond the Neon. Performing Arts Division • City of Las Vegas Department of
Leisure Services
El Consejo Municipal de la Ciudad de Las Vegas los invitan que acompañen al
Alcalde Pro Tem Gary Reese *a las ¡Fiestas Decembrinas!*
Sábado, 16 de diciembre, 2006, 5–8 P.M.
Disfrute de este festival con su familia, amigos y la comunidad entera.

- *Santa Claus*
- *Canciones tradicionales*
- *Entretenimiento en vivo*
- *Antojitos de venta*

Todos están invitados

Entrada Gratis

Para más información, llamen al 229-1515
East Las Vegas Community / Senior Center
250 N. Eastern Avenue
www.artslasvegas.org
www.lasvegasparksandrec.com

But here is the confusing part. If you were to survey public librarians and ask them what their prime duties are and what responsibilities they are tasked with completing on a daily basis, what do you think the responses would be? In public libraries, I would venture to say that we all agree that we are there to serve the customers who walk through our doors; to help people find information; to offer resources that might assist them, and to offer programs to meet their needs. If a Spanish-speaker were to visit her local *notario público* and say, "My husband and I are having issues at home. Our relationship is going south. Please guide or counsel us," the *notario público* would offer them counseling and information. Now, if this person were to come to a local library in the United States with the same question, what do you think the librarian's response would be? They would probably point them to area of the library containing relationship books and/or share names of local agencies that might assist them. However, that Spanish-speaker is looking for advice, not a referral.

Some of us learned in library and information science programs that we should not share personal beliefs and that we should only point these patrons to the appropriate portion of the collection or hand out information that they might use. But Spanish-speakers look to librarians for more advice than where books are on the shelves and what other community agency will help them. If they don't find the help they are looking for at the library, they will go back to their community and tell their peers about their experience. If the Spanish-speaking community feels it cannot trust the library or turn to librarians when they are in need, they will not utilize its services. This is why it is so important to communicate with Latinos on their cultural level and gain their respect and trust.

These examples highlight the differences between the expectations of the Spanish-speaking community and the way librarians currently conduct business. If we don't embrace the reality that Spanish-speakers tend to prefer advice over referrals, librarians will be doing an injustice to the Latino community as well as to themselves. We must value social interaction skills and personal connections and follow the golden rule of treating others as we would like to be treated. You may struggle with the concept that you will be considered an expert since librarians are used to pointing out where to find advice rather than offering advice themselves. Personal empathy and sincere concerns will help meet the perceived needs or expectations of direct assistance.

The following is a great example of how one private company reframed their product to be more youth-oriented. A July 2005 *Business 2.0* article titled "Hipper Than Thou" professes that "plenty of companies need to make old products seem new again, but few have pulled it off more divinely than Bible publisher Zondervan." The Bible has been a best-seller for centuries. Yet Zondervan, the world's biggest Bible seller, has experienced double-digit growth the last two years by repackaging the Bible, effectively turning it into a youth-oriented lifestyle accessory. Consistently the top performer in the HarperCollins publishing group, Zondervan owns 27 percent of the $1 billion Christian book market. "Young people today may not go to church," says Brian Scharp, vice president for Bible marketing at Zondervan, "but religion is important to them. We have to make it relevant." Here's how the company has proven that no product is too old or too familiar to be born again.

This "how" chapter has highlighted some of the most common examples and approaches to serving the Spanish-speaking community. This approach is important not only to reaching Spanish-speakers, but to any new type of constituency that libraries hope to reach.

This chapter has hopefully painted a picture of how to introduce and encourage the use of library services to Spanish-speakers. The focus of the three main issues, translation, transcreation, and the example of the notary public, demonstrate that serving this segment is somewhat complicated. My question or challenge to you is, how can we serve a distinctly different cultural group with approaches that were originally meant for another target audience? The easy road is to just apply those old approaches and hope that they work, even though they haven't worked so far. Or we may take the road less traveled and reeducate ourselves by reframing our approaches and messages. Since Spanish-speakers are not frequent users of libraries when they arrive in the United States, we must find ways of bringing our services to their attention. We must reach out to them in their communities and speak to them in their language, both linguistically and culturally. Reaching out to Spanish-speakers will be discussed in the next chapter, which will outline best practices that go against conventional wisdom.

FURTHER READING

Flight, Georgia. "Hipper Than Thou." *Business 2.0* July 2005, 6 (6): 1, 56.

CHAPTER 7

Reaching Out to Spanish-Speakers

It is not about knowing your customer. It's about your customer knowing about you.

—Jack Trout, *The Power of Simplicity*

This chapter looks at what outreach is and what it entails. The focus of outreach is to conduct library business in a nonlibrary setting. Outreach moves out the library and into the community to find those people who for various reasons are not willing to come into the library itself, but need the resources of the library.

Outreach serves the dual purpose of showcasing products and services and establishing good community relations. Its main goal is to explore and market libraries in less traditional settings. Outreach may be considered unorthodox as it an activity that most libraries have not done before.

"Siting" is the strategy of finding a location where you can get the best return on your investment. It is also the art of making decisions as to where and when to be present in the community. For example, if your local school is having a parent-teacher meeting for Spanish-speakers at the same time when the library is offering bilingual story time, you will need to decide at which event your staff will be present. These are hard decisions to make. You may continue to offer the bilingual story time, but be aware you are missing an opportunity as well. Find out when the next meeting is going to take place and be sure to schedule accordingly.

When conducting outreach activities, members of the Spanish-speaking community will find the library's presence to be both formidable and celebratory. They will be excited that someone is taking a concerted interest in helping them to become successful and knowledgeable. Outreach has the potential to be one of the library's most rewarding activities, but only if you are in the right place. As we have discussed in previous chapters, Spanish-speakers tend to reside in neighborhoods where they can satisfy all their needs for utilities, clothing, and groceries. At this stage in their development as residents of the United States, library services are not considered one of their most pressing needs. The objective of outreach is to let Spanish-speakers know that libraries provide services they should be capitalizing on.

There are two parts to outreach in Spanish-speaking communities. The first is showing up at events, and the second is speaking to the people. We will take a close look at the best ways to go about both. The intention of both techniques is to introduce and encourage the use of library services, but the impact should be that you deliver what you promised and stay in touch with the people with whom you have become affiliated.

One of the main keys to a successful outreach initiative is quite simple—just show up. Show up at as many events as possible that are relevant to the Spanish-speaking community. During these community events, when the librarian is intermingling with the Spanish-speaking community, it is very important to offer people a handshake and not a handout.

COMMUNITY EVENTS

There are several reasons why it is optimal to reach out to people on their own turf and instead of inside a library. When you reach out and deal directly with the community, you are showing that you have an interest in the community's events and fairs. By attending these events people will be able to ask and receive one-on-one answers and have personal interactions. This way you will be able to explain directly to the community member how the library works, in a neutral environment free of perceived threats. One of the most effective ways to introduce and encourage the use of services to Spanish-speakers is to provide them with a sample of what they may find within your library. This approach is effective for various reasons, but mainly in that they will be able to experiment with your services where they are most comfortable and then make a choice as to whether the services are relevant to them or not. Like any social or cultural group, when outreaching, promotional giveaways are great at catching their attention as it will draw them to your booth or table. Most promotional pieces work well, but as most libraries find themselves in financial uncertainty, mood pencils with your libraries name are inexpensive items that children, teens and adults will find interesting.

If your community has a decent number of Spanish-speakers, there are bound to be events offered by other social services agencies or by the Spanish-speaking community itself. Nothing is more powerful than to network with representatives from other agencies as they are trying to reach the same segment of the community. Sometimes the best way to become involved is to join up with a Spanish-speaking resident expert who has been involved in community outreach for quite some time.

The second activity involves being invited to speak to a group of individuals in the community. This will be determined by how active you have been in the community. If you have been a stakeholder within your service area or township, you might be a regular speaker at assemblies and community events. These entities will invite you back to reinforce the usage of libraries and hopefully to let people know about new resources as they are available. In small towns it might be at the local school or church. In cities, there is a greater variety of places to speak. Librarians in bigger towns face many social issues. As there are likely to be many more services available, the library should have an abundant amount of information that shows the library is knowledgeable of the resources that exist and that they will help their constituents succeed, whether they require Alcoholics Anonymous or Catholic Charities.

Allow me to share with you some personal experiences of what groups have invited me to speak at their events. One of my most frequent appearances has been at an organization called the Family Leadership Institute. The Family Leadership Institute is a grassroots entity whose curriculum aims to educate parents on how American society functions. They are taught that they have the right to attend school board meetings and share their concerns. They are trained on the importance of journaling. They are exposed to community speakers who talk about what services are available. They are also exposed to the importance of community involvement.

Twice a year I am invited to speak about leadership within the Spanish-speaking community and the importance of reading and library usage. The organizers of the Family Leadership Institute have identified some of the trustworthy people within social services entities and place on them the responsibility of mentoring and motivating this group of parents. I was selected to be among this group based on my previous involvement in the community, my track record.

Other entities that have me speak to them constituents are English as a Second Language (ESL) classes at the local school district. They ask me to speak about library services and what impact library services can have on their lives. The thing to remember is that anyone can be asked to present these presentations. What makes a presentation unique are the skills and talents of the speaker. If you recall the list of traits found in chapter 1, you will remember that Spanish-speakers appreciate humor. I usually break the ice with a few jokes to make everyone feel at ease. A popular starter is "Why does a dog wag its tail?" The answer is, because the tail cannot wag the dog! Once you and the audience feel at ease with each other you may start your more serious discussion, not a canned speech but a dialogue about library services.

If you are new to outreach and do not know how to start receiving invites or are having a hard time identifying agencies where you may find captive audiences, my advice is to be patient and start by slowly getting involved with community committees. A point that I like to emphasize frequently is that libraries are in the library business, but they are also in the community business. Pay a personal visit to the agencies that you believe serve Spanish-speakers and pick up their literature. You will be surprised at how social agencies depend on other social agencies to distribute their message. These flyers or brochures will often have contact information that you should follow up with. Gradually, you will be noticed as an individual and library staff member who is interested in serving the Spanish-speakers and in their well-being and will end up as part of a circle of individuals and agencies dedicated to servicing Latinos.

When you or a library staff member is invited to speak to Spanish-speakers, you will have already broken ground and gained some trust from other people in the community and you know you are seen as a respected individual who has the best interest of the Spanish-speaking community in mind. What is even more important than being invited to speak is the message that is to be delivered to the group of Spanish-speakers. What is said during this discussion will be a turning point that can make you and your library seem even more relevant than ever, or just be seen as a simple front on the library's behalf.

The messages that have proven most successful when reaching out to Spanish-speaking communities all center on being successful in the United States. This also entails focusing on community issues before library issues. Instead of focusing on what the library has to offer, concentrate on how you may assist the community. The two messages that you need to share and reinforce are that one does not make a long journey to fail and that if your audience members want to be successful, they need to affiliate themselves with successful people. After you have stressed these two concepts, you must repeat and repeat them as the Spanish-speaking community thrives on motivation.

It is important to share these messages, as we have discussed, in ways that are culturally relevant. Below are two inspiring stories of Latinos who had difficult beginnings but who became prominent members of society. These stories are a great source of motivation when speaking to community groups. These and the stories of many other individuals were found using databases from Gale such as Biography Resource Center and Contemporary Hispanic Biography, which should be readily available in most public libraries. The Biography Resource Center has a Biographical Facts Search that allows you to search by many criteria, but the fields that should assist you in finding important people are those of nationality, ethnicity, and gender. If you were to select "Hispanic Americans" under "Ethnicity" and then select "Female," a list of respected and influential Latinas would surface.

Many of these individuals have parents with similar backgrounds to those of the Spanish-speakers you are trying to reach. The electronic version of *Contemporary Hispanic Biography* contains biographical entries on notable Hispanics/Latinos from a variety of fields. Two individuals that you may want to discuss are Antonio R. Villaraigosa and Rosario Marin.

ANTONIO VILLARAIGOSA

In 2005, Antonio Villaraigosa became the first Latino mayor of Los Angeles, California in over 100 years. Mr. Villaraigosa grew up in a single-parent family after his alcoholic father abandoned his family. At the age of 15 he suffered partial paralysis due to a tumor on his spinal column. The next year he was expelled from high school for fighting. During this period of not being able to play sports and not being in school, Villaraigosa found refuge in his local library, where he would read the works of Shakespeare. Despite the many odds that were against him, he went back to school and earned a law degree. He went on to make a name for himself by organizing people with the United Farm Workers and United Teachers Los Angeles and being politically active. One of the qualities that his mother instilled in him and his three siblings is a love for books. He credits this with why he is so well read. During one interview, Villaraigosa was asked what he considers his ethnicity to be, and he responded with "I am an American of Mexican descent." This touching story might resonate with many Spanish-speakers and would likely appeal more to them than trying to advance a library offering. Once they are captivated with such powerful true stories, you may attest that libraries are part of the path to success. In this case you make your points relevant by first sharing a story that will appeal to your Spanish-speaking audience and then proceed from there. Now let's look at another powerful story.

ROSARIO MARIN

Rosario Marin was the 41st treasurer of the United States under President George W. Bush. She was the first Mexican-born U.S. citizen to receive this post. When Rosario was 14 her parents told her that they were moving to the United States. She was adamantly against moving because she was about to celebrate her *Quinceañera*, her 15th birthday. Marin's mother convinced her by telling her that they would return to Mexico to celebrate her *Quinceañera*. They did end up going back to celebrate this festivity with all of their friends and family. When Marin was enrolled in school she did not pass the standardized test and as a result was written off by teachers as being mentally disabled. But after studying hard and sacrificing much, she graduated from high school with honors. Marin continued her education, started a family, and pursued a career. She became a city council member in Huntington Park, California, which eventually led to her becoming mayor of that city. Due to her political involvement, she became noticed at the national level.

Now here is the key to Marin's story. While Marin was staying up late completing her college assignments, there was always someone always next to her—her mother. Marin's mother did not speak English and could not assist Marin academically. But she was there to support her daughter by keeping her company and always offering to cook or provide drinks. Rosario credits much of her success to her mom.

When speaking in public to Spanish-speakers, you have the opportunity to challenge them by asking hard questions, such as "Are we doing the things that will make us successful, such as making the choices that Villaraigosa and Marin did? If not, why not?" These stories are motivational, provocative, and stimulating. The Spanish-speaking community will be inspired to know that others before them have been successful and that they too can achieve the same greatness. But in order to do this, they need to learn English, be model citizens, be great parents, vote, and become familiar with the many social services available to them, including the library.

OUTREACH: AN EIGHT-STEP PROCESS

Outreach can be seen as an eight-step process. The process is defined clearly in the following table of attributes (Table 7.1) to focus on when conducting outreach efforts. Outreach is the activity that will invite Spanish-speakers to the library. It also your chance to control what first impressions they have of the libraries, as a first impression is indispensable.

Many librarians don't see the need for outreach as they believe that Spanish-speakers will not use their services. These people are probably right. Why should a person use the library if they have never been courted and if it does not offer the right services, programs, collections, and staff? It makes perfect sense. Would you go to a place where you do not feel welcomed? The purpose of outreach is to gain a greater

Table 7.1: Outreach Defined

O	Outreach feeds on outreach. The more outreach you do, the better you will become at it and the more people will come to value the library.
U	Understand the complexities of Spanish-speakers. The one-size-fits-all concept does not apply here. You must do some research if you want to reach people.
T	Time is of the essence. It usually takes about three years of constant involvement before you notice your hard work pay off. Don't give up before then.
R	Reach with urgency. Libraries cannot afford to wait. Act now as this generation and the following generation will dictate the success of this country.
E	Everyone is your customer. Make a concerted effort to familiarize people with your services and programs on their home turf. The customers will follow.
A	Attitude is of the utmost importance as a positive first impression will determine whether people feel put off or welcomed.
C	Care for the needs of Spanish-speakers, even if they are not library-related. This means working toward creating public value within this segment by addressing their needs.
H	The Human factor needs to be in place. Remember that people enjoy talking and interacting. Take this element away and you are back to square one.

understanding of the needs, expectations, values, and beliefs of Spanish-speakers and then return to your library and incorporate what you have learned and observed. It is most important to deliver on the promises of things that you said you would do.

I hope that I have made a credible case for having outreach as an integral part of your institution. Like many of our services, support of certain services is predicated on budget. Unless you are in a fortunate library system with plenty of public support, you will run into the same dilemma that many public librarians face, the lack of funds to incorporate new services and staff. If that is the case in your area, I recommend something that Jim Collins, author of *Good to Great*, stresses—that a "stop-doing" list is more important than a "to-do" list.

Like any public library, we feel that every single effort is in the best interest of our patrons. Even when we discuss what to eliminate, we believe that everything we do is essential and therefore not subject to elimination. Yet, when we add more to our plate, no portion of our existing workload is reduced. This is a detriment to our patrons as our services suffer as we spread ourselves too thin. Seriously consider doing away with some services that do not work as well as they have in the past and focus on emerging services that will ensure that libraries continue to create public value.

One of the best examples I have heard of how a library director can budget for outreach and serving Latino communities was shared during the 2008 Public Library Association Annual Conference. Kathryn Ames, director of the Athens Regional Library System in Athens, Georgia, sponsored a program titled "Bridging the Gap: Library Services to Latinos." During this great workshop, she and other library staff members associated with their grant-funded program shared their experiences. The following is the program blurb: "Lifelong learning, family literacy, basic library services, art classes, art exhibits, and a visiting artist comprise this 3-year IMLS grant. The panel will discuss designing and implementing their model for the community, building new relationships, using an advisory board to keep services on track, and teaching new skills." Part of the grant included purchasing a trailer for the library. They hired a teacher to teach staff Spanish. They traveled to Mexico, which opened their eyes as to the Latino culture. For more information about this great initiative, contact the Athens Regional Library System in Athens, Georgia and ask for Miguel Vicente or Kathryn Ames.

Once you have been out in the community tooting your horn about how great your library is and how the services and programs that you offer will benefit Spanish-speakers, it will be time to actually deliver on the services you promised. The following chapter will highlight essential services that are considered a must in public libraries. The mentioned services have a proven success record and can be implemented in public libraries of any size.

FURTHER READING

Collins, Jim. 2001. *Good to Great*. New York, NY: Harper.

CHAPTER 8

Essential Services for Spanish-Speakers

This book has asserted that the best way libraries can become and remain relevant is to offer culturally related services. Libraries are no longer simple places where people come only to conduct research, browse collections, study, and have quiet meditation. The library has evolved from offering only these services toward being a place where people may connect with their world, where users may explore topics that might interest them, and where they may interact with others. It is a place for students to complete their homework assignments. It is a place where everyone can be assisted in making choices. Librarians like to seek out information, but most people like to just come across it. This is why social networking sites are so popular. At the same time, it is important that libraries continue to offer traditional research services.

Spanish-speakers are very loyal, so once you find them, it is your task to keep them as users. One way to determine if libraries are actually creating public value is to contemplate whether you are satisfying or managing the needs of the Spanish-speaking community. Even though there are generational, cultural, personal, and economic shifts within the Spanish-speaking community, the number of Spanish-speakers will remain constant or will grow. If you are not aware of the numbers, Table 8.1 gives some statistics on the number of Spanish-speakers in the U.S. Hispanic population.

Table 8.1: Hispanic Population Estimates (5 Years of Age and Over)

Year	Total	Spanish-Speaking	(as Percent of Total)
		Hispanic Population	
2005	37,324	27,797	74
2015	48,686	34,446	71
2025	61,341	40,191	66

(Source: U.S. Hispanic Population Projections. Hispanic USA)

Knowing that Spanish-speakers will be part of our communities now and in the future means that services will need to be in place to make the library a prominent institution in their lives. It is already a proven fact that Spanish-speakers prefer institutions and establishments with Spanish signage, literature in Spanish, and workers that speak Spanish. Therefore there are a few simple and effective things you will need to do to make the library experience both productive and memorable. Lori Klein, from the National Library of Medicine in Bethesda, Maryland, shared with us the most-viewed topics in both English and Spanish according to the MedlinePlus Web site. Table 8.2 below showcases the results.

One way of ensuring that the services that are needed and are actually implemented is to have a measurement tool. In libraries, this comes in the form of a strategic plan. What is even more important is to ensure that there is a cultural diversity component to the plan. Once the plan is in place, it is vital that you or other management personnel ensure that all components are carried out. The following are three examples of strategic plans that have an element that addresses diversity or Spanish-speakers. The Fort Worth Public Library long-range strategic plan had an objective stipulating that "by 2005/06, 1,000 people who speak English as a second language will attend computer classes sponsored or co-sponsored by the library that are offered in their native language. 90% of those users will indicate on a post-class evaluation form that the programs met their needs." The San Francisco Public Library strategic plan aimed to "increase representation at street fairs and other community events to encourage neighborhood involvement and to promote library services throughout the year. Incorporate into outreach strategy to be developed and implementation begun by 2004/05." The Oceanside Public Library strategic plan aimed to "work with ethnic and cultural groups to showcase community diversity." A cultural services librarian was to "plan at least two cultural events per year from Oceanside's African-American, Filipino, Latino, Samoan, and Asian communities" and would also "recruit community contributions for library displays related to cultural programming."

A noticeable and prominent Spanish-language section is mandatory. The placement of this collection will facilitate the usage of library resources. The question here is not if libraries should have a Spanish collection, but where in the library it should be situated. Much literature is available on the subject of starting Spanish-language collections. This area should have strategic signage and offer popular and classic titles in several formats. The types of materials offered should include books, magazines,

Table 8.2: MedlinePlus Go Local Top-Viewed Topics

English-Speaking Community	Spanish-Speaking Community
Herniated disk	Pregnancy
High blood pressure	Sexually transmitted diseases
Diabetes	Diabetic diet
Back pain	Diabetes
Pregnancy	Brain and nerves
Ovarian cancer	Anatomy
Sexually transmitted diseases	High blood pressure
Diabetic diet	Digestive diseases
Anatomy	Heart disease
Herpes simplex	Skin conditions
Birth control	Attention Deficit hyperactivity disorder (ADHD)
Chronic obstructive pulmonary disease (COPD)	Herpes simplex
Parkinson's disease	Asthma
Human papillomavirus (HPV)	Thyroid diseases
Multiple sclerosis	Knee injuries and disorders
Skin cancer	AIDS
Staphylococcal infections	Blood, heart, and circulation
Hives	Anemia
	Endocrine system
	Gall bladder diseases

music, video, instructional ESL materials, and *fotonovelas*. If you don't know the best way to start, most jobbers have start-up collection builders to assist librarians who are building or upgrading their collections. Getting in touch with the major vendors is a good start as they have resident experts in specialized departments.

One thing I have observed that works quite well is a "quick-pick" section in the circulation or self-check vicinity. These sections are great as they are a place to put high-interest books in one area so that patrons don't have to browse countless numbers of shelves. These quick picks should have subjects that are of interest to Spanish-speakers, such as relationships, parenting, how to be successful, and cooking, arranged in no particular order. Make sure they stand alone and are not interfiled with English materials. Label the shelving unit in Spanish and you will see your circulation statistics skyrocket.

Other simple proven tactics are to have display racks with Spanish classics, new books, and bestsellers. If you cram these three types of books into the general Spanish collection, they will get lost in the clutter. A Spanish-speaking staff member may be best qualified to pick out books for this shelf. If there is no Spanish-speaking staff, an adult volunteer would do a good job of selecting titles. Posting flyers in your library seeking such assistance is a good first step toward finding such a volunteer. Once you have a network of contacts from the Latino community in place, they might even suggest people to you, but you will have to tell them what specifically you are looking for.

There are many ways to highlight a Spanish collection. Signage and images should be properly posted. Posters featuring Latino celebrities are great ways to point out your collection. ALA Graphics offers George Lopez READ posters (these may be purchased online from www.ala.org). Librarians should also consider creating similar posters themselves featuring local community figures. Striking a balance is important because librarians need to think nationally but act locally.

The best resource for Spanish-language resources, services and collections in the library community is *Críticas*, a sibling publication of *Library Journal. Críticas: An English Speaker's Guide to the Latest Spanish-Language Titles* is a monthly review of Spanish-language books produced by *Publishers Weekly, Library Journal*, and *School Library Journal*. Published online monthly, *Críticas* presents an authoritative one-stop source for English-language reviews of new adult and children's titles from the national and international Spanish-language publishing world. Two print issues a year, one in June and one in November, complement the online version of the magazine. The monthly online issues are free to the public. You do not need to register to access any of the articles, reviews, or archives.

MAGAZINES

You should also offer magazines in Spanish. According to a report by Packaged Facts titled "The U.S. Hispanic Market: Looking into the Future," the top 10 general-market magazines read by Hispanics (not Spanish-speakers) are *Reader's Digest, TV Guide, Better Homes & Gardens, National Geographic, Women's Day, Time, People, Sports Illustrated, Newsweek*, and *Cosmopolitan*. The top 10 Hispanic titles and their respective circulation (in thousands) are *Ser Padres* (510.0), *People en Español* (416.8), *Readers Digest Selecciones* (279.3), *Latina* (243.7), *Vanidades* (109.7), *TV Y Novelas* (102.8), *Christina La Revista* (86.0), *Cosmopolitan en Español* (55.9), *Newsweek en Español* (46.7), and *Furia Musical* (22.4).

The marketplace has a wealth of Spanish-language magazines. One way of determining which magazines you should keep in the library is by paying a visit to a local Latino establishment such as a supermarket and reviewing the titles being sold there. A list of some common magazines found in Latino establishments can be found in Appendix A.

Adding Spanish-language books and magazines can be a daunting task if you are doing it by yourself and for the first time. I highly recommend using jobbers in your quest for finding Spanish-language materials. You may face several challenges in creating a collection without a jobber's assistance; for example, books and magazines sold only in the native country, a limited number of books in print, exclusive vendor rights to selling materials, and materials taking a long time to arrive. In addition to the jobber, it is a good idea for you to become familiar with the Spanish-language book market. Of course you may read articles on the subject, but the best way to gain experience is to attend the Feria Internacional del Libro in Guadalajara, Mexico. The American Library Association has a special program to help defray the costs for people who want to attend this wonderful book fair.

The Latino Institute for Development, Education & Responsibility (LIDER) offers a seminar titled "In Search of the American Dream, A Program for Public Libraries" (http://www.lider.org/libraries.asp). This program is designed to unite private and public sector efforts to provide public libraries with Spanish-language books and audio books that teach the life skills required to ensure personal and professional success. Life-skills titles (how-to, self-help, information to help set up a business) are among the most commonly requested titles by Latinos in public libraries. The seminar is open and free to all library patrons and is heavily promoted by the media and local Latino groups. This program creates a perfect forum for attracting Latino families to the library and announcing ongoing library programs and services. The "In Search of the American Dream" program reaches many Latinos, particularly newly arrived immigrants who are in the earliest stages of their educational process. These people are in search of information, on a quest to discover just how they can succeed in the United States.

A final tool that might be of some assistance is the "Guidelines for Library Services to Spanish-Speaking Library Users" created by the Library Services to Spanish-Speaking Community and approved by the Reference and Users Services Association Board of Directors in January 2007. For the complete guidelines, visit www.ala.org and run a search for "Guidelines for Library Services to Spanish-Speaking Library Users."

One way of ensuring that your library is providing the right services is by developing a service plan for your library. The Las Vegas Clark County Library District in Las Vegas, Nevada, headed by Executive Director Daniel L. Walters, has service plans for each of their urban branches. Below you will find a service plan that was developed for a library situated in a predominantly Spanish-speaking neighborhood. It was created a few years ago, so most of the statistics are not up to date, but the format of the service plan is what is most important. You will find the complete East Las Vegas Library service plan in Appendix B.

Now that you have read this far into this Crash Course, and if you are willing, able, and ready to making the leap into providing library services to Spanish-speakers, you will find in the following chapter invaluable proven programs that have been in place at institutions that have a track record with serving Spanish-speakers. It will offer the most up-to-date program development and also highlight some programs that are common throughout the country. The programs that are featured are but a handful of great programming that currently exists. Even librarians at small libraries or small library systems who have previously been conservative in targeting Spanish-speakers should come away from this chapter with better ideas for program development. Remember, it may be a small step on your behalf to offer services, collections, and bilingual literature, but with the implementation of programming, you will be showing a vested interest in serving the needs of Spanish-speakers.

RECOMMENDED VIDEOS

Bienvenidos a las Bibliotecas del Condado de Washington [Welcome to the Libraries of Washington County]. 2001. Washington County Cooperative Library.

Bridging the Digital Divide in the Spanish-Speaking Community. 2004. Colorado State Library. Library Video Network.

CHAPTER 9

Successful Programs for Spanish-Speakers

This chapter will offer the nuts and bolts of program development for Spanish-speakers. As we discussed earlier, librarians coordinating programs for Spanish-speakers need to understand the exclusivity of the culture of Spanish-speakers from Latino perspective as this will guarantee a rapport when putting programs into place. In order to create public value, these programs need to assist with a contemporary need. Before you begin, you must find out what is most important to your clientele, not what you perceive as important. Some customary values of Spanish-speakers are family and community, education, and having fun.

Currently, there is no one single entity that owns the literacy initiative in the Spanish-speaking community. If librarians begin to approach literacy from a cultural perspective, they could be the most successful entity offering literacy and educational programs. Librarians are in the learning and idea business and as such, should offer these types of programs. When it comes to programs relating to reading literature, Spanish-speakers are most likely to participate in programs that are of the most interest to them. Two recommended programs, "People and Stories" and book discussion groups, are described below.

One of the best programs that offer training and a curriculum is People and Stories/*Gente y Cuentos* (www.peopleandstories.org), a grassroots humanities program designed to create an enjoyable and enriching experience with literature for those who are not presently reading independently. In this program, short stories of literary merit are read aloud and discussed using a well-developed method that draws upon readers' life experiences to help them understand basic literature. I have personally offered this initiative in my library, and even though the turn out wasn't as high as we had hoped, the quality of discussion and conversation was well worth it. Participants shared, reflected, and, most importantly, left with a desire to read more.

A book discussion group or *club de lectores* is another way of appealing to this segment of the community. The key to being successful is to promote your program heavily and keep it at a consistent schedule and location. A bookmark should be created with the books that are going to be discussed over the course of the year. This comes in handy when patrons miss a meeting. They will then be able to see which book is next on the reading list.

The name of this book discussion group should remain in Spanish, as *club de lectores*. Many book discussion groups in English have names that speak to the type of literature or genre that they read. This approach will not go over well with Spanish-speakers. The scope of material that is discussed is important, however. For the most part it is has been my observation that books written by renowned authors from Spanish-speaking countries work well.

Each library has a different instrument for measuring success. A library could be measured as successful by the number of its participants or by how much it meets a need in the community. Something important to think about is that if you are new to serving Spanish-speakers, attendance at your events will initially be low. But this is to be expected. Don't be discouraged. Attendance will gradually increase. Do not allow low attendance to discourage your staff from continuing to offer library programs. If attendance continues to be low, however, you may want to reconsider the topic of your program.

Some potentially good program topics are health, beauty, education, telecommunications, finance, interviewing, culture, and religion. Below you will find some examples of ways to create programs around these topics.

Health-related programs encompass weight loss and fitness. Spanish-speakers also want to know of ways that they may be healthy and in good physical shape. A representative from a group such as Weight Watchers may conduct the program and touch on good eating habits and proven practices.

Beauty programs will attract women who are interested in looking their very best. They will also be interested in learning how they can assimilate into the larger community so they do not stand out as different.

Education topics can include how adults may advance their children's educations. This might require the adult to become familiar with the many educational resources in the area and to learn how the school system works.

Telecommunications topics could include how to purchase and use electronic components such as computers. Research shows that young Spanish-speakers embrace technology. Teaching the adults in the household why that is will make them more knowledgeable about why their children want these gadgets.

Spanish-speakers want to be financially successful in the United States, so finance is a topic of much interest to them. Topics could include teaching them the benefits of purchasing a home, opening bank accounts, and saving for a college education.

An interactive interviewing workshop coaches patrons on how to present and sell their talents. Interviewing programs can help participants learn how to apply for a job and how to prepare for the interview. You should have some mock interviews to allow for practice. The news of your success in helping people become employed will spread very quickly.

Cultural programs can include topics such as preparing for a *quinceañera* and observing National Hispanic Heritage Month. National Hispanic Heritage Month should offer a slate of programs that people from all walks of life may attend to learn more about the history, contributions, and culture of people of Latino heritage.

When scheduling programs you need to be careful not to exclude too many cultures. For example, Cinco de Mayo is only relevant to people from Mexico. If you only offer Cinco de Mayo programs you might alienate Latinos from other cultures. Communities with a large Spanish-speaking population may have representation from many different cultural groups, all of whom should be catered to. What has happened with Cinco de Mayo is that it has become popularized by mainstream businesses, not necessarily as a time to observe the importance of the holiday, but by drinking alcohol and enjoying as much guacamole and chips as possible. At the same time do not discontinue it, as the holiday is a source of pride for those individuals that observe it.

Religion, when discussed in a library, should not focus on any particular house of worship. Instead, religious programs should be seen as a cultural component, as Spanish-speakers are for the most part religious in some way. For a great example of a religious cultural program, see the examples of best practices detailed below.

The following best practices programs have proven successful at libraries throughout the country. They are described below in terms of their benefit to the community, how the event is promoted, whether they partner with any other organization, lessons learned, and how they advanced the library among this segment of the community.

DRAMA DE LA PASIÓN—JESÚS DE NÁZARETH

Run by: Jose Arias, General Director. Drama de la Pasión—Jesús de Názareth, Las Vegas, Nevada.

Description of program: Drama de la Pasión—Jesús de Názareth is a five-act theatrical performance that presents the events leading up to Holy Friday. The program touches on the public life of Jesus, His last supper, His sentencing, His road toward The Light, and his death and resurrection.

Benefit to the community: The general director of this passion play recruits local talent each year and gives them the opportunity to participate in the play. Actors spend many hours practicing and rehearsing, forming a community in the process. The library sponsors a number of live presentations to the community which normally last three to four hours. These programs take place during Holy Week.

How it was promoted: Information is posted on the Spanish version of the library's Web site, posters are created and posted throughout the library, and flyers are created that patrons may take home. The play participants distribute posters and flyers among the establishments that they frequent. They also distribute them within their social networks.

Partnerships: In this case, the library did not seek partners. Most of the grass-roots efforts were carried out by the group members. The group did seek assistance from the local Colombian association to promote the program and lobbied every single Spanish-language media outlet in the area.

Lessons learned: Sponsorship occurred out of coincidence. A library staff member was at a mall outreach event when the play's general director approached the staff member about sponsoring the program. After an initial meeting at which the general director gave a convincing presentation about the merits of the program, the library moved forward with sponsoring the event. It has been five years since the start of this joint venture and the library has been proudly sponsoring the program every year since its inception. The lesson learned was that there are times when you have to advance a service and program at face value and hope that it is well received. In this case it has been and community members are await the theatrical presentation every year.

How did it advance the library among this segment of the community? The partnership between the library and the general director has resulted in much publicity to the library. Members of the passion play are exposed to the library quite frequently and become aware of its many services and programs. Event goers are introduced to a facility in the community with which they might not be familiar. Periodically, members of the passion play are willing to do additional presentations on a variety of topics, both recreational and educational.

TEC DE MONTERREY, *HABILIDADES BÁSICAS DE INFORMÁTICA* (BASIC INFORMATIONAL SKILLS)

Run by: Sol Gomez of Pima County Library, Tucson, Arizona.

Description of program: A 21-week online course entirely in Spanish provided by the Tecnólogico de Monterrey, a prestigious university in Monterrey, México. Students first learned the basics of computer use over a total of about 12 hours, meeting once a week for a month. Once they knew the basics, students would register for Tec de Monterrey's online course, *Habilidades Básicas de Informática.* The online course consists of seven modules covering the following topics: Introduction to the Computer, Software, Internet, E-mail, Microsoft Word, Microsoft PowerPoint, and Microsoft Excel.

Benefit to the community: Empowerment would be the most noticeable benefit to the students. Before taking the online course, students feared the computer. Even if students did not complete the entire 21-week course, students felt confident using the computer on their own. Students would also visit the library more often to check their e-mail or just browse the Internet. Several students went on to attend Pima Community College.

How it was promoted: In its initial phase with the library system in 2005, Telemundo and Spanish-language radio stations promoted the program. As time progressed, the only marketing technique that continued the survival of the program was word of mouth.

Partnerships: Pima County Library in Tucson, Arizona partnered with the Honors College of the University of Arizona. Students involved in the Honors Civic Engagement Teams (HCET) contributed to Tec de Monterrey by assisting in teaching the course and offering tutoring hours throughout the week.

Lessons learned: It is essential to create a roster with names and phone numbers to make reminder phone calls about the scheduled class. These phone calls helped in increasing student retention. With the phone call system in place, students began calling and notifying staff when they could not attend class. Prior to the phone system, students would sign up for a class and then a week later, when the class was scheduled, not show up. Constant communication is a key factor in student retention. It is also crucial to continue to meet physically as a class on a regular basis even though it is an online class. Working together as a team not only helped with the course itself, it helped build relationships among students. Students who were more advanced would help other students.

How did it advance the library among this segment of the community? Many students were surprised that a librarian would be doing this kind of work in a community. Librarians are no longer viewed as people behind a desk; they are actually viewed as literary and educational representatives of the community.

Additional comments: The Tec de Monterrey program has helped many people in the Spanish-speaking community. One way to make this computer program even better would be to have everything offered locally. Instead of communicating and trying to solve online issues either by e-mail, long-distance calls, or mail, everything should be able to be resolved locally.

¿IR A LA UNIVERSIDAD? ¿QUIÉN? ¿YO?/GOING TO COLLEGE? WHO? ME?

Run by: María T. Palacio of the Lee County Library System, Fort Myers, Florida.

Description of program: College information for teens offered in Spanish and in English during the fall of 2006 and winter of 2007. Description on flyer is as follows:

> Es emocionante graduarse de la escuela secundaria, pero decidir
> que hacer después, puede ser intimidante. Maria Fernanda Torres,
> especialista en desarrollo estudiantil del Edison Collage, ayudará
> a los estudiantes entre 10mo y 12vo grado planificar su futuro.
> Igualmente se discutirá sobre las maneras y pasos para entrar
> a la universidad y las diferentes formas de pagar los estudios
> universitarios.

High school graduation is an exciting time, but deciding what to do afterwards can be scary. Maria Fernanda Torres, Edison College Student Development Specialist, helps 10th through 12th graders plan their future as she discusses ways to enter and pay for college.

Benefit to the community: Benefits to the community included the provision of information in the native language and from a person who has been in a similar situation. These presentations provided parents and children with access to information they could not always get from overextended guidance counselors in high schools. The community also benefited from seeing that the library offered materials on college entrance exams and scholarships that could be borrowed from the library.

How it was promoted: Staff created flyers, press releases, and posters. María T. Palacio, the Multicultural Program coordinator, visited the high schools closest to the library locations, offering information about the presentations and gathering guidance counselors' contact information. Palacio then sent flyers directly to the counselors to promote the program. As a result of this outreach, two teenaged Cuban students attended one of the sessions. Their counselor had alerted them to the presentation. The young ladies had immigrated to the United States very recently and while they were earning very good grades, they had not been able to pass all of the sections of the Florida Comprehensive Assessment Test (FCAT). Nevertheless, they wanted to find out how to get into college.

Torres, the presenter, also wrote an article about her work at Edison College and her partnership with the library. The article appeared in *Gaceta Tropical*, the local Spanish-language weekly, around the time that the presentations were scheduled to take place. Palacio also appeared on the local Univision affiliate's *Enfoque Hispano* show to promote this and other programs.

Partnerships: The Lee County Library System (LCLS) partnered with Edison College, a former community college, now the largest college in the area offering several four-year programs. At a women's conference sponsored by the Southwest Florida Hispanic Chamber of Commerce, the library's deputy director had the opportunity to hear Torres speak. The deputy director then asked Palacio to try and contact Torres to brainstorm ideas about partnering with her and the college. Palacio met with Torres and created a schedule to offer college information presentations in English and in Spanish.

Lessons learned: Almost 70 people attended the sessions. The LCLS learned that there is a great need for this type of information in the Latino community, especially for parents who have recently emigrated to the United States. The attendees varied; some had lived in the United States for a number of years but had recently moved to Florida and were unsure of the college entrance process in this state. Others were recent immigrants whose immigration status and that of their children was not yet permanent. They too needed information about what to do since the opportunity to win scholarships is sometimes limited by immigration status.

How did it advance the library among this segment of the community? The college information presentations advanced the presence of the public library in the community. People who came learned that they could come to the LCLS for information. Many people shared news of the presentation with others and even people who could not attend called asking for information. Palacio in turn referred them to Torres, who was able to provide information to these callers. Many attendees also borrowed materials on the subjects of college entrance and scholarships, which were on display during the presentations.

Additional comments: Torres is a dynamic speaker and was very upfront and honest with attendees. During the presentations she shared the incredible story of how she had immigrated to the United States only five years earlier. She entered high school and knew that she wanted to go to college, but because her immigration status had not yet been favorably resolved, she didn't qualify for many scholarships. She did not let this deter her and decided to speak to the different Latino leaders and business groups to ask for help in funding her education. She earned a scholarship through the SWFL Hispanic Chamber of Commerce and attended Edison College. After earning her associate degree there, Torres transferred to Eckerd College in St. Petersburg, Florida. Upon graduation she was offered a job at that college and at Edison College to recruit minority students. Torres decided to give back to her community and returned to Ft. Myers to help minority students there. She has since moved to another state where she is hopefully doing the same kind of work. Because of these presentations, several students found out how to apply for dual enrollment at their schools through Edison College. Palacio knows of at least one student who started in the program the fall of 2007. At the end of several presentations, Palacio went on to offer brief tours of the library focusing on the Spanish-language collection and on materials relevant to education.

QUEENS LIBRARY HEALTHLINK

Provided by: Loida Garcia Febo of the Queens Borough Public Library.

Description of program: In 2007, the American Cancer Society estimates that each week in the borough of Queens, New York, 182 people will be diagnosed with cancer and 68 people will die from the disease. The Queens Library HealthLink initiative was developed to place libraries at the center of an innovative new effort designed to help medically underserved communities throughout Queens access free cancer information, early detection screenings, cancer treatment resources, and other life-saving services. The Queens Library HealthLink is a collaborative initiative of the Queens Library, the

American Cancer Society, the Queens Cancer Center of Queens Hospital, and Memorial Sloan-Kettering Cancer Center. It is a five-year, federally funded research project based in Queens that will explore the potential to partner with libraries as a vehicle for community health outreach to fight cancer. HealthLink includes:

> Free or low-cost cancer screening services through the New York State Healthy Living Partnership and their mammogram van; access to cancer treatment at the Queens Cancer Center regardless of ability to pay or immigration status; American Cancer Society educational programming offered at community libraries; cancer core collections in English and Spanish; programs on early detection for you and your family; creation of Cancer Councils, groups composed of community leaders and members to increase cancer awareness within the libraries' service area; conduct surveys within the 20 participating library neighborhoods throughout the five-year project in order to measure the impact of Queens Library HealthLink programs; provide specialized staff with expertise in health and community organizing (HealthLink Specialists) to work with neighborhood residents to identify community health priorities and needs.

Benefit to the community: With a population of more than 2.2 million people (U.S. Census, 2000), the borough of Queens is the second most populated borough in New York City and one of the most ethnically diverse counties in the United States. Some 47 percent of the residents in Queens are foreign born; 53 percent of its residents speak a language other than English at home; and 27 percent of its residents speak little to no English. The burden of cancer in Queens continues to remain a vital health issue. Queens has a higher rate of late-stage cancer detection compared with the rest of New York state. In all major cancer sites, the Queens Health Network has seen an increased likelihood of late-stage diagnosis and increased rates of mortality. The rate of late-stage detection found at Queens Health Network for breast cancer is almost three times the national average, and for prostate and colorectal cancers, it is nearly twice the national average. HealthLink's goal is to increase access to cancer screening and care among medically underserved communities in Queens. The Queens Library HealthLink will build on the already strong relationships that the Queens Borough Public Library has within the neighborhoods it serves.

How it is promoted: The program was launched on January 17, 2007, at the Jackson Heights Community Library with participation from Memorial Sloan-Kettering Cancer Center, American Cancer Society, and Queens Cancer Center of Queens Hospital, a choir from an elementary school and many representatives from New York City media. Posters in Spanish and other popular languages spoken in Queens were created to publicize the program and sent to all participant libraries. The flyers of the educational programs and the schedule of the mammogram van are sent to the media, community libraries, and outside agencies. Queens Library's marketing and communications department sends press releases in English and Spanish to publicize the events.

The partners of the library on this project assist in this joint effort by e-mailing electronic flyers to their contacts. The HealthLink Community Outreach Specialists has compiled a mailing list of agencies that provide information about cancer awareness and serving cancer patients along with family and friends. The library also has a mailing list of Latino organizations in Queens. On a daily basis, library staff put flyers inside books when they are checked out.

Partnerships: The American Cancer Society, the Queens Cancer Center of Queens Hospital, and Memorial Sloan-Kettering Cancer Center.

Lessons learned: Libraries can successfully partner with outside agencies without jeopardizing the trust deposited in them by community members concerned with immigrant status. Many organizations are available and willing to serve all members of the community and to provide services regardless of ability to pay or immigrant status. Partnering with agencies and organization leaders within their fields helps to enlarge the scope of services that can be offered. Periodic meetings between partners are necessary to review practices and processes and straighten out glitches along the way.

Coordination of services among HealthLink and the library's different units is needed to secure parking for mammogram van, equipment, meeting rooms, and for the creation and printing of flyers. Creation of bilingual printed material is vital for effective communication with the community. Training of HealthLink Community Outreach Specialists in library matters provides the knowledge needed to refer customers to the appropriate library unit according to their needs, be they English classes, after-school programs, or other programs and services in Spanish.

How did it advance the library among this segment of the community? Librarians have a social role within the community, and by helping reduce health disparities within our libraries' service areas, we demonstrate our commitment to society. Making educational programs, cancer screenings, and core collections about cancer topics available to Queens residents who otherwise might not have access to them is a way of ensuring access to information for all members of our community. The official HealthLink Web site can be found at http://www.queenslibrary.org/index.aspx?page_nm=QL_HealthLink.

INTERCAMBIO/LANGUAGE EXCHANGE

Run by: Rita Jimenez and Ana Schmitt of the Multnomah County Library, Portland, Oregon.

Description of program: An Intercambio or language exchange is a volunteer-run one- to two-hour library session to which the public can come and practice speaking English and Spanish. Time is provided for conversation in both languages.

Benefit to the community: At Intercambio, both English and Spanish native speakers are able to come together with a common goal and help each other. It is a great opportunity for people to practice the language they are learning in a comfortable and nonthreatening environment.

How it is promoted: Intercambio has taken place at other libraries prior to the Multnomah County Library. It was brought to the Multnomah library by a community member and library volunteer. She arranged access to the media through public service announcements at a local Spanish TV network. Promotional materials in Spanish and English were distributed at library locations, through the library's extensive social service agency contact list, and to family-friendly and Spanish-friendly businesses. When reaching out to the community, we continue to use the library's extensive contacts with community agencies serving Latinos, such as local businesses, schools, community fairs, and community colleges to promote this program. We also added the Intercambio information to our Web site Event Finder program and to our Spanish Web site as well.

Partnerships: The same volunteer hosted Intercambio at other libraries as well and requested collaboration from different community partners to get it started. The Multnomah County Library has been supporting this program for many years now and will continue to offer it.

Lessons learned: It is important to have plenty of volunteers before starting the program. We recommend starting with six and meeting with them to do some planning. Let them know what is expected, such as promoting the event, arranging the room, being there on the assigned day, and so on.

How did it advance to the library among this segment of the community? Intercambio brings people into the library who otherwise wouldn't come. It also welcomes them to continue to use the services that participants learn about by visiting the library. People can use library materials, including books, encyclopedias, and maps as prompts for conversation during any particular Intercambio session.

This chapter has provided information on program planning for Spanish-speaking clientele and has also given some specific examples of programming provided in other places. While many of these programs take place in large public library systems, the same types of programs could be offered in smaller libraries, with a little assistance. The advancement of the library in your community makes it all worth the effort.

CHAPTER 10

Marketing to Spanish-Speakers

This chapter discusses how library marketing to and public relations efforts with Spanish-speakers need to use completely different approaches from those used with the general population. These approaches are essential even for a larger library with a public relations department. Marketing to Spanish-speakers should be a strategic initiative rivaling traditional library marketing. Spanish-speakers want messages created just for them, as they know that they are different from the general population. It is very important to create graphics and images that have appropriate emotional appeal.

Any marketing or advertising initiatives to Spanish-speakers must focus on the family unit, not on the individual, as is usually the case for the general market. In Spanish-speaking households, decisions and activities are carried out as a family unit, and librarians need to consider this complicated concept. One example frequently referenced by librarians as an issue is when more than two individuals go on a library computer at the same time. The library's policy might state that only one or two people are allowed per computer. You may still explain the rule and reasons for the rule and then enforce your computer usage rules. However, even though they are not following protocol, it helps understand where they are coming from culturally. When Spanish-speakers use computers as a "crowd," they are for the usually looking for information valuable to the entire group.

Several features should be paramount to any marketing and promotional pieces. It is a proven fact that the best marketing in the Spanish-speaking community is conducted in Spanish, on its turf, and with a message that contains culturally relevant information and images. Using visuals such as maps and humor that also informs patrons about the library's services is a great start. Four "F" words that ought to be used in your Spanish promotional pieces are "free," "fun," "family," and "food"—in that order. These are four "F" words only in English; in Spanish they translate to *gratis*, *disfrute*, *familia*, and *comida*.

Felipe Korzenny, author of *Hispanic Marketing: A Cultural Perspective*, states on the topic of Hispanic marketing that "in the United States, however, the masses of consumers need communication that is high on information and low on image. This is because they are inexperienced as consumers and eager to learn the basics about products." This concept applies to marketing for libraries. As you undertake the process of offering services to Spanish-speakers, you need to help them learn how they may empower themselves with the services that are currently being offered. The following is a sample newspaper ad that would definitely capture the attention of Spanish-speakers:

SPANISH

Todos los servicios y programas son gratuitos y están abierto al público. Para mas información llame al (123) 456–7890. Ofrecemos libros, revistas, música y computadoras; talleres de computadoras con certificado; cursos de ingles; ayuda con tareas; personal que habla español; y servicios para toda la familia incluyendo niños y jóvenes.

ENGLISH

All of our services and programs are free and open to the public. For more information, contact us at (123) 456–7890. We offer books, magazines, music, usage of computers, computer classes, English as a Second Language classes, homework help, staff that speaks Spanish, and services for the entire family to include children and teens.

At this time we will review a great marketing piece from the private sector that is both culturally relevant and advances the purpose of the product. We will then apply the lessons learned to a library scenario. Let's take a close look at a Toyota Tundra commercial that appeared on a Spanish-language television station. This is the how the commercial goes: A Spanish-speaking couple in the 20–39 age range is having dinner. The pregnant female comments that the avocado she is eating does not taste anything like her grandmother's avocados. In the following scene there is a countryside where you can see a empty truck navigating the roads. The next scene has the same truck returning, its truck bed covered with a tarp. Then we are shown the couple having dinner once again, the pregnant female saying that these avocados do taste like her grandmother's, while the husband smiles. In the next scene, the grandmother comes out of her house to find an empty hole in her yard. "Where is my avocado tree?"

she says. The final scene is of the husband standing on the front porch of a house with another man (perhaps the pregnant woman's father) looking at the truck. The commercial ends with: "People will see you differently."

Nowhere does the commercial state how much horsepower this vehicle has. It doesn't share the many features of this vehicle. In fact, it doesn't divulge any features that might make it different from its competitors. It solely relies on cultural elements with a minimal amount of spoken words. This commercial ran for an entire year. This same approach is transferable to a library setting. Let's remind ourselves of the cultural characteristics of Spanish-speakers and apply those to the library world.

Most librarians who have aspire to reach Spanish-speakers want to highlight the library's collections, services, and programs. But it must be done with the cultural characteristics of Spanish-speakers in mind. For example, instead of portraying a Spanish-speaker reading in your library, why not have this same person reading in his own family room with a group of people in the background doing homework or playing a board game. This will capture the Latino values of community and family. Culturally speaking, it shows closeness within the household, while also advancing the activity of reading. The text in the piece should say something to the effect that you can enjoy learning about something wherever you are.

Keywords that have been successful in other marketing efforts include *nuestra gente*, "our people." With the phrase *nuestra gente*, Spanish-speakers are not isolating themselves, but it is reflecting upon their culture and their community in the United States. These types of phrases will create a bond between your patron and your service. You can pick up on these types of phrases by reading books and articles on the subject of Hispanic marketing or about Latino culture. The bibliography includes some recommended titles.

We have addressed some of the things that we should be doing. Let's now review a few things that you should not do. This is very important because if we do not address the things that we should not be doing, we will continue to do them when they are either not productive or make no impact on the intended audience. Most of the things on the "do not do" list center around stereotypes. Some overused stereotypical Latino clichés include the Latin lover, the macho man, the Spanish grandmother (*abuelita*), the servant, and the man with a sombrero and a burro. Once certain images or aspects of any culture are used too frequently they become stereotypes, and the list above contains just a few that have survived the test of time. While each of the stereotypes mentioned has some basis in reality, they will mostly be dismissed by Spanish-speakers as type-casting. The burro and sombrero man will resonate mostly with non-Spanish-speakers. This is an image that is mostly used for tourist souvenirs.

If you need guidance on what is considered a positive or negative stereotype, ask your community contacts. Make sure you have a good pool as part of your research. Something that has been useful to many librarians is to form a Community Advisory Committee. This committee is comprised of members of the community with representation from varied cultural groups, including individuals from social services providers who have dealt with Spanish-speakers and who may speak to their needs based on their experience. You must be active in the community to become familiar with such individuals. Sending letters or e-mails out to individuals with whom you do not have a rapport will likely not generate a good response. A good tactic is to find a trusted source in the community who is also a library advocate and have this person show you around and introduce you to the many individuals and groups that presently serve Spanish-speakers.

If you want to further your library's presence within the Spanish-speaking community, you need to make a concerted effort to bridge the cultural gap. In many cases the best marketing is done by the patrons and not by the library. In the meantime, practice what works and avoid the errors that will set you back. Remember that marketing to Spanish-speakers is a relationship that takes time to mature.

FURTHER READING

Korzenny, Felipe. 2005. *Hispanic Marketing: A Cultural Perspective.* Burlington, MA: Elsevier.

CHAPTER 11

Internet Resources for Spanish-Speakers

Teaching your Spanish-speaking community about computer use is an excellent service to offer. Many in the community are computer literate and a Web site is a good way for you to reach them. This chapter explains what to put onto your library's Web site as well as more about Internet usage.

A well-crafted Spanish site as part of your library's Web page will serve as an information portal for the many great services and programs that you offer as well as a clearinghouse for the many services that exist in other agencies in your community. The purpose of your offering Internet sites is to bring community members into the library as well as to other places of interest that will create public value. Links on your site should emphasize the local resources that exist and have an relevance to the day-to-day issues of Spanish-speakers. Your Web page may also focus on sites that are national in scope, such as government information.

Internet usage among Latinos is growing by 26 percent annually. It is hard to tell what percentage of these users are solely Spanish-speakers. Regardless, a well-organized, informative, and relevant Web site is essential and well worth the money it costs. When you launch a Spanish Web site, partnering with other sites such as those of your local social services providers and education institutions or agencies is a great way to advance the importance of the library's presence. Also be sure to offer a Spanish-language help section, frequently asked questions (FAQs) section, and site navigation guide.

Your site does not need to be entirely translated or transcreated. Much of the English information can be enjoyed by Spanish-speakers. Only certain components need to be translated. FAQs, cultural programs, the library's policies, and other important information are but a few things that merit translation. Below are some FAQs that should be addressed in Spanish.

Frequently Asked Questions

English	*Spanish*
How much do you charge for your services?	*¿Cuanto cobran por los servicios bibliotecarios?*
Are you related to the police?	*¿Estan relacionado con la inmigración o Immigration?*
What services does the library offer?	*¿Que servicios ofrece la biblioteca?*
What are the library's hours?	*¿Cuando está abierta la biblioteca?*
How do I obtain a library card?	*¿Cómo obtengo la tarjeta de la biblioteca?*
May my child receive a library card?	*¿Mi hijo/a puede conseguir una tarjeta de la biblioteca?*
How long can I keep checked-out materials?	*¿Por cuanto tiempo puedo pedir prestado los recursos y materiales de la biblioteca?*
How many items may I borrow?	*¿Cuantas cosas puedo pedir prestado?*
What happens if I return an item late?	*¿Que pasa cuando regrese los recursos y materials tarde?*
Do you offer ESL classes?	*¿Ofrecen clases para aprender inglés?*
Do you accept donations?	*¿Aceptan donaciones de libros?*
How may I reserve a library room?	*¿Cómo puedo usar o reservar un cuarto en la biblioteca?*
Do you offer services for children?	*¿Tienen recursos y servicios para niños?*
How do I reserve a computer?	*¿Cómo puedo reservar una computadora en la biblioteca?*
Do you have Internet access?	*¿Tengo acceso a la red en la biblioteca?*

If your Web site has a section for visitors or those who are new to the city, a directory with the following listings would be very helpful:

- airports
- community centers
- police and fire departments
- radio stations

- shopping centers
- educational resources
- employment centers
- government offices
- health services
- social services
- hospitals
- department of motor vehicles
- consulates or embassies
- newspapers
- television stations
- transportation
- utilities
- board of elections

An "Ask a Librarian" feature will be successful if people learn how to use it. According to Docutek, A SirsiDynix Company, Ask a Librarian assists "librarians directly with patrons online in real time as they guide them through Web sites and other online resources." Do not eliminate such a feature if after a few weeks or months it shows little or no usage. Be aware that this library service will be used, but it may be with limited success.

Subject matter comprising a great library site should include and present the following information:

- upcoming events
- displays of multicultural images
- local resources
- how to access the library catalog
- available databases
- locations of nearby libraries
- partnerships
- what is new at the library and in the community

It is also important that these resources be presented clearly; this information should not be hard to find. Your Web site should have a clear link (such as "*Español*") that will direct visitors to the Spanish portion of your library's homepage.

The following few pages contain information about databases for public libraries and listings of links that you might consider adding to your Spanish-language Web site.

SPANISH-LANGUAGE DATABASES AND RESOURCES

The following information has been taken from each resource's respective Web site.

Consulta 2.0

Thomson Gale has partnered with the premier Spanish-language reference publisher, Grupo Ocèano, to offer high-quality reference works for students, professionals, and general readers on crucial subjects such as careers, health, history, and literature. Consulta 2.0 (http://www.gale.cengage.com/pdf/facts/consult.pdf) gathers reference material, primary sources, and journal articles into one easy-to-navigate Web-based product for students and general researchers. In addition, Consulta 2.0 includes a graphical timeline as well as a map center, anatomical atlas, and literature library. Completing this generous selection of material, much of which has never before been available in the United States, Consulta also includes more than 6,200 full-color photographs, maps, and artwork. To meet the demands of both Spanish- and English-speaking researchers, the revised Consulta 2.0 has incorporated several key enhancements, including an interface that can easily switch between English and Spanish.

¡Informe!

Expand your library's services to meet the needs of the growing Hispanic population in your community with ¡Informe! (http://www.gale.cengage.com/pdf/facts/inform.pdf). Created exclusively for Spanish-speaking users, this full-text electronic reference tool is the first system to provide indexing, images, and full text of popular Hispanic magazines, not just translations. Also included is a thesaurus and interface that are uniquely designed for Spanish-speaking users. ¡Informe! "thinks" through every query in Spanish. Terms and thesaurus are based on the expressions Spanish-speakers commonly use, allowing users to easily navigate through the database without experiencing inaccurate search terms. ¡Informe! also features title annotations in both English and Spanish to help non- Spanish-speaking staff to assist users easily. Students of Spanish as well as nonnative speakers can also easily access ¡Informe!'s resources through this bilingual approach.

Noticias en Español

Accede Noticias (http://www.newsbanklibraries.com/libraries/product.cfm?product=28) provides Web-based access to the complete electronic editions of more than 20 Spanish-language newspapers published in major U.S. cities from Florida to California. It also includes the complete electronic editions of newspapers and tens of thousands of current and archived full-text articles from other news sources across Argentina, Brazil, Chile, China, Columbia, Ecuador, Mexico, Peru and Spain. All news and information content is written in Spanish rather than translated from other languages. With this specialized, value-priced resource, you can inexpensively extend the domestic or international news coverage provided by their *America's Newspapers* or *Access World News* collection. Accede Noticias can be cross-searched with these collections, and it shares the same user-friendly interface. However, it can also be browsed, searched, and purchased individually.

La Cumbre en Español

La Nueva Enciclopedia Cumbre (http://www.scholastic.ca/education/library/ encyclopedias/cumbre.html) online is a 6-million-word repository of text and images maintained by the encyclopedia's editorial and technical staff. It is published by Grolier Online, an imprint of Scholastic Library Publishing.

Salud Para Todos

This database (http://support.epnet.com/knowledge_base/detail.php?id=2226) is a full-text consumer health resource written entirely in Spanish. Designed specifically for those seeking information about health and medicine, the content in Salud Para Todos includes all articles that appeared in the original Oryx Press print version of *Información de Salud para los Consumidores*, essays and articles from government and health agencies, articles from Nidus Publishing's *Well-Connected* series, and articles from the *Clinical Reference Systems* collection. The full-text articles contained within the database were selected from over 300 publications and sources created by over 50 research associations and national institutes. Each article is associated with one of 48 main categories including substance abuse, cancer, mental health, contraception, infectious diseases, and many other key health areas. Salud Para Todos helps public libraries provide their Spanish-speaking researchers with comprehensive health information.

MedicLatina™

MedicLatina™ (http://www.ebscohost.com/thisTopic.php?topicID=106&market ID=2) is a unique collection of medical research and investigatory journals from renowned Latin American and Spanish publishers. This Spanish-language database contains a complete table of contents and PDF full text for nearly 100 peer-reviewed medical journals in native Spanish. A wide range of topics are covered, including neuroscience, cardiology, nephrology, biomedicine, clinical research, pediatrics, human reproduction, clinical pathology, cancer research, and hematology. Titles include *Revista Medica del IMSS, Revista Mexicana de Patologia Clinica, Boletin Medico del Hospital Infantil de Mexico, Archivos de Neurociencias, Revista Biomedica, Veterinaria Mexico, Salud Publica de Mexico, ACIMED*, and more.

Fuente Académica™

Fuente Académica™ (http://www.ebscohost.com/thisTopic.php?marketID=1& topicID=71) provides PDF full text for more than 330 scholarly publications covering areas of academic study. Content is provided in Spanish from respected publishers worldwide, including *Revista de Arquitectura, Estudios Sobre Educación, Revista de Estudios Hispanicos, Comunicación y Sociedad, Revista de Ciencia Politica, Revista Historia,* and more.

Latino American Experience

Wide-ranging and easy to use, the Latino American Experience (LAE, http://lae. greenwood.com/Default.aspx) is the first ever full-text database focusing on the history and culture of Latinos living in the United States. LAE's content spans from the pre-Columbian indigenous civilizations of the Americas through the Spanish and Mexican settlement of much of what is now the United States, to the triumphs and challenges facing present-day U.S. Latinos.

Featuring more than 150 titles (including award-winning titles from Greenwood, Praeger, Arte Público, Columbia University Press, and other imprints), 1,500 images, hundreds of primary documents, Spanish-language content, a timeline, and 225 vetted Web sites, LAE is the most comprehensive digital resource to date to focus exclusively on Latinos. In addition, LAE's "Origins" section features both ready-reference and in-depth information about the history, culture, and customs of the people of Latin America, the Caribbean, and the Iberian Peninsula.

Tutor.com

Live Homework Help *en Español*

Live Homework Help *en Español* (http://www.tutor.com/) provides your Spanish-speaking patrons with academic assistance in their native language. In addition to the program components outlined above, this service also includes:

- Bilingual Classroom—bilingual live homework help interface
- Bilingual Tutors—professional tutors fluent in both Spanish and English (includes bilingual tutors in Latin and South America)
- Bilingual Math and Science Support—bilingual Spanish/English assistance in math and science Sunday every day from 1:00 P.M. to 10:00 P.M. PST. Additional social studies subjects are offered upon request
- Special Promotional Tools—additional introductory four-color marketing materials

WebJunction Spanish Language Outreach Program Overview

WebJunction's Spanish Language Outreach Program (http://www.webjunction. org/do/Navigation;jsessionid=433C83C521A4BCEF3703164659610BC9?cat egory=10555) will help equip you with knowledge and resources to reach out to

Spanish-speakers in your community and increase your patrons' access to technology. The program's workshops provide you with information about proven marketing techniques, understanding cultural differences, providing technology training, and partnering with local community organizations serving Spanish-speakers.

The program begins with a Training Institute during which trainers hired by participating state libraries will become familiar with the program's curriculum. Following the Institute, trainers will utilize the curriculum to deliver workshops in their state. When you attend one of these local workshops, you will learn how to develop an outreach action plan based on the curriculum and activities presented in the workshop. In addition to providing on-the-ground workshops, WebJunction is fostering an online community of interest made up of library staff committed to serving the needs of Spanish-speakers. The program utilizes discussion boards for sharing ideas and resources among participating libraries, trainers and other WebJunction users. The program's resources are available at http://www.webjunction.org/spanish.

The Web sites identified in this chapter are for Spanish-speakers. Some of the emerging or forthcoming Web sites that will be popular among second-generation Latinos are shown below. The first few Web sites are highlighted with a description.

MTV Tr3s (http://www.facesofmtvtr3s.com) is a new bicultural entertainment destination rooted in the fusion of Latin and American music and culture.

SiTV (http://www.sitv.com/) is an English-language Latino cable network that caters to today's young English-speaking Latinos who consume English media, but still want shows that speak to their Latino roots.

Mun2 (http://holamun2.com) is part of Telemundo cable, the cable division of the Telemundo network, which is providing young Latinos with a unique, new entertainment option that reflects their lifestyles.

LATV (http://www.latv.com/) is the nation's first bilingual music and entertainment network. They are a pioneer in bicultural youth broadcasting and offer an array of programming that is original, exclusive, and live, targeting Latinos 16 to 34 years old.

CHAPTER 12

Findings from Surveys of Spanish-Speakers

This chapter examines data that were collected in two ways. The first come from a Mexican question-and-answer game show similar to *Family Feud*. The second are data collected from community events that were attended by Spanish-speakers. The results from these often informal and nonscientific studies indicate that Spanish-speakers have mixed feelings about reading. The responses of Spanish-speakers to the questions posed reveal some interesting points from the perspective of the Spanish-speaking community, and are some of the most important findings pertaining to reading among Spanish-speakers and Latinos.

Let's first look at what respondents recently said about reading on a Spanish television show titled *100 Mexicanos Dijieron*, a game show equivalent to the *Family Feud*. The following were their guesses as to the top reasons why Mexicans don't read. According to this show, the top four answers were:

1. *Tiempo*—not having enough time
2. *Flojera*—being lazy
3. *Aburridos*—books are boring
4. *Les da sueño*—they fall asleep

If I were to ask you this question without providing you with the four answers, what would your four answers look like? Would they resemble the answers from this television show? Many times library staff members make erroneous assumptions as to why Latinos don't read based on myths that are perpetuated by the media's negative coverage of Spanish-speakers. Another belief held by many librarians is that Spanish-speakers have no experience with libraries in their native countries. While some of these assumptions are based on truths, the problem occurs when these assumptions turn into stereotypes that all Latinos are unfairly subjected to. According to *Marketing to Hispanics* by Terry J. Soto, "A survey conducted among Spanish-dominant Hispanics indicates that 86 percent of households purchased at least one book a year, while 29 percent bought ten or more adult books a year in Spanish, pointing to a Spanish-language book market of more than $350 million annually." *La Opinion*, the largest and longest-running Spanish-language newspaper in the United States, has a daily circulation in Southern California second only to the *LA Times*. These facts highlight that many Spanish-speakers do, in fact, read.

What might be of particular importance to librarians are the data in the following tables. These were gathered from a survey of reading preferences among Spanish-speakers titled *Reaching the U.S. Hispanic Market*, conducted by the Direct Marketing Association in 2006. The questions asked correlated to four factors: language preference, place of birth, age, and education. This in-depth analysis of first-generation Spanish-speakers shows that the percentage who read only in Spanish is 34 percent, while those who read only in English is 30 percent. A high percentage of those who were born in the United States read only in English, while a higher percentage of those born outside the United States read only in Spanish. Age did not seem to affect the percentages greatly. Education seemed to be a factor. Readers who had only gone to high school were much more likely to read only in Spanish.

The library profession in the United States has not conducted a thorough report on the reading preferences of Spanish-speakers. Therefore we need to rely on research papers from the private sector.

These survey findings were compiled while attending grassroots cultural events where the majority of the event goers were Spanish-speakers. For example, some surveys were completed during a citywide Día de los Niños event. Others were conducted while visiting the Mexican Consulate, and the remaining were conducted through a network of community peers. Below are the questions that were asked and an abbreviated summary of the most common responses, in no particular order. Many of the

Table 12.1: Do You Prefer Reading in …?

Language Used for Reading	Percentage of Total Respondents
Spanish only	34%
Spanish preferred	10%
Both equally	17%
English only	30%
English preferred	9%

Table 12.2: Place of Birth

Language Used for Reading	Born in the United States	Born Abroad
Spanish only	8.0%	58.8%
Spanish preferred	1.8%	19.9%
Both equally	21.3%	14.2%
English preferred	13.5%	2.3%
English only	55.4%	4.9%

Table 12.3: Age

Language Used for Reading	<25	25–34	35–44	45–54	55–64	>65
Spanish only	15.6%	32.3%	35.7%	30.4%	33.8%	37.8%
Spanish preferred	5.4%	12.7%	10.4%	11.8%	7.3%	8.5%
Both equally	25.1%	15.9%	19.5%	12.7%	18.5%	16.5%
English preferred	10.2%	8.5%	5.0%	10.8%	7.9%	8.5%
English only	43.7%	30.7%	29.4%	34.3%	32.5%	28.7%

responses may come as a surprise, while others concur with what we already know. What is most noteworthy is that these responses were documented by people from the community.

1. What is the main reason why Latinos do not use libraries?

The top eight reasons Spanish-speakers gave as to why they do not use libraries were: lack of time; lack of English; lack of library promotion; lack of bilingual staff; that people don't know the services are free; that they are not interested; that they have other family priorities; and that libraries are too far away. Some of these responses are applicable to many parts of the country, while some may not be. If you take a close look at the reasons why Spanish-speakers do not use library services, they all seem like reasonable and valid responses. What this author has noticed is that when librarians try to reach Spanish-speakers, that often they do not take into consideration some of the reasons stated above, particularly people's lack of time and their family priorities. Librarians are compelled to introduce and encourage the use of library services, but they sometimes lose perspective of the bigger picture.

2. What do you propose that the library do to encourage the use of library services by the Latino community?

The top five responses were: more promotion of services; promote that there are bilingual staff; highlight that many of the services and programs empower and educate; partner with school personnel; and to send library material with them so they would have a more complete collection including many formats. The Spanish-speaking community still feels that there is a big gap between them and library services. In all of my research, only in a few cases have librarians pointed out and stressed to the

Table 12.4: Education

Language Used for Reading	Some High School or Less	High School Degree	Trade or Technical School	Some College	College Degree	Some Grad School or Degree
Spanish only	63.7%	31.4%	31.0%	14.3%	12.1%	–
Spanish preferred	7.5%	12.7%	17.2%	6.1%	5.2%	–
Both equally	10.6%	20.3%	15.5%	20.4%	20.7%	75.0%
English preferred	5.3%	6.5%	10.3%	12.6%	13.2%	–
English only	12.8%	29.1%	25.9%	46.5%	48.9%	25.0%

Spanish-speaking community that they have staff to meet their needs. The "*Se habla Español*" sign is not good enough. It has been overused and quite honestly, you have to go through a maze to really reach a Spanish-speaking staff member or representative. The Spanish-speaking community has an idea of what it takes to succeed, but they are in dire need of programs and services that highlight how they may familiarize themselves with the new culture that surrounds them. Becoming familiar with programs such as the Family Leadership Institute, which has a proven curriculum to help accustom Spanish-speakers to their new surroundings, is important.

3.   In your opinion, what message should the library reinforce to Latinos?

The top five replies were: usage of computers; having bilingual staff; encouraging patrons to have confidence in using library services; using themes that educate and empower Spanish-speakers; and letting Latinos know that the library is theirs as well.

Gaining the attention of and marketing to Spanish-speakers can be quite complicated. Some private sector companies are doing a very good job of advertising by using messages that are culturally relevant. Once you have heard the opinions of Spanish-speakers in your community, it is important that you honor some of the above-mentioned replies. Some of these findings may be universal and your "remedy" may be using the word "confidence" or "*confianza*" in your communication with these patrons. Tell the Spanish-speaking community to have confidence in using your library services, as it is their library, too. In Spanish there is a common phrase, "my house is your house," or "*mi casa es su casa*," which you should translate to include your library. A well-devised message should be personalized to incorporate a more down-to-earth meaning and not a standard, corporate-sounding, nonrelevant point.

4.   What is the most important subject matter for Latinos?

The top three answers were ESL, computers, and immigration. Other important secondary issues mentioned included education, health, security, their traditions, employment, family, and U.S. society. Two of the top three answers, ESL and computer use, are common among library services and programs. Programs relating to immigration and the secondary subjects are less common. Yes, storytelling might fall inside the scope of education, and many cultural programs fall under the scope of Latino traditions. But for the most part these library initiatives are seasonal and offered periodically, instead of on a constant basis that will generate long-term dedication.

Each community has different needs. A very important and contemporary subject for Spanish-speakers is immigration. Are librarians doing enough, or anything at all, to address this need? If not, they should be. Since librarians are well positioned to lend a hand to Spanish-speaking communities, librarians ought to embark on hosting interactive immigration forums that will educate their patrons about the laws so that they are better aware of this sensitive issue.

5. What media outlets are the most commonly used by Latinos to learn about community events and services?

The top four media outlets in order of importance were television, newspapers, radio, and the Internet. The media outlets should come as no surprise, but the order of importance should. Each media outlet has its strengths. Television ranks high as it is something that whole households may see at the same time. Newspapers have information that people may take with them and share with family and/or friends. The radio is synonymous with music and talk shows that might pass on vital information. The Internet is starting to emerge as a source where Spanish-speakers may retrieve information about community events and services.

Depending on what part of the country they are in, communities with small Spanish-speakers may not have all of these media outlets available. Even if there are only one or two types of media available, take advantage of them, as Spanish-speakers are in dire need of information that will assist their community—the same community you are seeking to assist. In larger cities with larger Spanish-speaking communities, libraries will be competing with other social agencies for ad space or news about their services. That is why it is important to establish a relationship with reporters. For the most part, underrepresented groups use social networks the most.

6. Knowing and understanding what libraries currently offer, what services and programs would you like to see the library offer?

The top eight responses were: ESL programs, computer classes, motivational programs, bilingual staff, employment workshops, cultural programs (not only during National Hispanic Heritage Month), and programs on how to deal with teens. You will notice that many of these services and programs are ones that many libraries already offer. Libraries typically offer ESL and computer classes as well as cultural programs. What need to be added to the existing lineup are services and programs that motivate Spanish-speakers, as well as ones that teach parenting skills. Many Spanish-speakers already have jobs, but in their quest for a better life, they also want to have decent or better-paying jobs. You can motivate them while offering a interviewing skills workshop. I conduct interactive interviewing skills workshops where those attending are taught how to market themselves, respond positively, and research the company so that they enhance their interviewing aptitude. By the end of this workshop, Spanish-speakers feel more confident about their interviewing skills and are also motivated to aim for a better job. The beauty of this S.M.A.R.T. (which refers to <u>S</u>how up early; <u>M</u>arket yourself; <u>A</u>ttitude is positive; <u>R</u>esearch organization and/or business; and <u>T</u>ype application) workshop is that it is now being offered off-site at places other than the library.

7.   Do you think that reading is a habit among the Latino population? Why/why not?

The majority of respondents thought that reading was not a habit. The five top reasons why were: being too tired from work; being unfamiliar with libraries; lack of reading skills; preferring of television over reading; and having no education. The reasons given will vary in urban versus rural communities. Most Spanish-speakers from urban centers are familiar with the essential functions of a library. They might not necessarily take advantage of these services, but they do know that they exist and will use them when they have an urge to read. Most Spanish-speakers from rural areas are not familiar with the essential functions of libraries. Rural areas are where you would most likely receive these top five reasons why reading is not a habit.

When mingling with Spanish-speakers, it is important to share with them the importance of a print-rich environment. People who come from households that are rich in printed materials have proven to be more successful than those from households that do not embrace reading. A household with a print-rich environment is a household where reading materials are readily available. It means that there is always something to read, whether that be newspapers and magazines just lying around or having a formal library. When you show Spanish-speakers that they may have a print-rich environment using freely borrowed books from the library, they will change their attitude toward the library and view it as a place that can advance their educational and recreational reading interests.

8.   Did you enjoy library services in your country of origin?

A two-to-one ratio of respondents indicated that they did not use library services in their country of origin. Some of the excuses were that no library infrastructure existed; that libraries were scarce; that libraries didn't exist, were not nearby, did not have user-friendly hours of operation, and offered no programming. When Spanish-speakers first arrive in the United States and begin learning about our society, learning about the library is not a top priority. Either they do not know that libraries exist ,or they do not know how libraries can help them. One cannot think of using a resource that one does not know exists. This is why outreach is of the essence.

9.   What library services do you currently enjoy?

The top responses were: lifelong learning; computers; ESL programs; resources that meet their interests; friendly staff; a welcoming environment; children's section; and good signage. When the survey was conducted, we did not ask people if they were regular library users. Based on the answers to the questions, we are assuming that the respondents were somewhat familiar with the services and programs available, as their responses mirrored what is currently being offered. In order to keep some consistent patterns of services and programs, it is important that you continue offering the programs mentioned. Since these are a library's strength, continuing these tasks will ensure continuity for people who are currently not library users but who may be drawn to the library in the future. You will notice that a friendly and welcoming staff was much appreciated by Spanish-speakers. This is an indicator of great customer service. Staff must be sincerely interested in ensuring that patrons have a good experience, and librarians are seen as hosts. As we have already discussed earlier, Spanish-speakers are people-oriented and enjoy personal interaction during their library transactions.

10. What is your favorite book subject and why?

The top two subjects were religion and motivation, followed by cooking, health, history, metaphysics, traditional Latino authors, and how to prepare for the future. The top two subjects are important as they reflect the values, beliefs, and experiences of Spanish-speakers. Most Spanish-speakers are religious, but new research is highlighting the fact that Spanish-speakers are leaving the Catholic Church because they are unhappy with sermons that tell them they should live within their means and be happy with their current state of being. Other denominations are challenging that belief and stressing to Spanish-speakers that they should strive to be successful and challenge their current lifestyle. Motivation is also a top interest as Latinos seek guidance, encouragement, and direction from wherever they can get it to learn how to survive and succeed in this new setting. The books and seminars of Camilo Cruz are one of the many ways to cheer them on. For more information about leadership and the Spanish-speaking community visit El Exito (http://www.elexito.com, currently in Spanish only). I highly recommend Dr. Camilo Cruz's resources as he is a highly regarded national bestselling author and speaker. Being the author of several books in the area of personal development and leadership, he is a sought after in the United States and in many Latin American countries for his *Reaching the American Dream* lectures.

The responses to the *Reaching the U.S. Hispanic Market* library survey should provide you with some insight as to how Spanish-speakers feel about library services. But the responses have been abbreviated, and we still need to dig deeper. That is why conducting your own surveys or polls is imperative to understanding the needs of Spanish-speakers in your community and to offering services and programs that will create public value.

An important lesson from these survey findings is to assess and digest the results and see how transferable they are to relevant and responsive library services. A more elaborate study is needed to fully understand how Spanish-speakers feel about and perceive libraries, but until then, this abbreviated survey will highlight their most common insights and opinions.

At the same time, a survey of librarians about their insights and opinions of Spanish-speakers is also needed to highlight the similarities and/or disparities. This is important because if librarians do not share the same views as Spanish-speakers, it will highlight why Spanish-speakers are not receiving proper, fair, and equitable library services.

CHAPTER 13

Issues of Spanish-Speakers

No matter what part of the country you reside in, you are bound to observe some debate centered on the Spanish-speaking community. Some of the information you will hear on this subject is in fact legitimate, while some is unfounded. Many of the issues that are common to Spanish-speaking communities are worthy of debate and generate much passionate since they affect all sectors of society. When you translate community issues to library services, there will be additional topics that will need to be addressed. Four trends that I feel merit some serious dialogue are language, *biblioteca* (library) v. *libreria* (bookstore), retro acculturation, and the future.

LANGUAGE

The language you use to communicate with the Spanish-speaking community will impact how they perceive your institution. Although we have focused on the Spanish language, there are other variations of Spanish that will come into play when trying to appeal to Spanish-speakers. Some of these variations include "Spanglish," code switching, and Caló. These different idioms can be used as the Spanish-speaking community evolves and becomes more acculturated and/or assimilated. It is important to know the differences between these variations.

- Spanglish is a word in English given a Spanish connotation. One example is the English word "to park" and the term *parquear*. The correct Spanish word would be *estacionar*.
- Code switching is the art of going from English to Spanish without missing a beat. One example of a code switching sentence: *cuando yo puedo hablar* in English, and you are able to *entender lo que yo estoy diciendo porque*, you know both languages.
- Caló is a dialect where words are created, embraced, and made popular. Some common Caló words are *cantón* (house), *ranfla* (car), and *tramos* (pants).

Spanish-speakers have two schools of thoughts about using correct Spanish. Some believe that all marketing should be in correct Spanish, while many believe that you should be able to improvise and use idioms that are bound to echo with designated audience. In the Spanish-speaking community, it has been my observation that there is nothing wrong with employing Spanglish, code switching, and Caló.

BIBLIOTECA (LIBRARY) VS. *LIBRERIA* (BOOKSTORE)

Spanish-speakers respond to services and brands with which they are familiar. Since many Spanish-speakers are not that familiar with library services, we need to advance vocabulary that will resonate with them. Since they are not accustomed to library services in their native countries, we need to use terms that they will embrace while in this country. Conventional wisdom will and has reinforced the concept of using *biblioteca* when introducing and encouraging the use of library services. But the way you go about familiarizing the Spanish-speaking community with your service in a cultural context will determine your success.

According to Felipe Korzenny, author of *Hispanic Marketing: A Cultural Perspective*, "Vocabulary in Spanish regarding soap or coffee may have strong emotional associations as part of growing up in their own countries; however, vocabulary regarding banking or computers may be familiar only in English." Let's take simple vocabulary in both English and Spanish as an illustration. For example, some detergents and beverages have strong cultural relevancy as they are related to growing up in people's native countries; however, new words or terminology, such as libraries, computers, and financing, are words that are picked up in the United States and only familiar in English. I am a proponent of only using the word library and not *biblioteca*. If such a theory sounds revolutionary, that is because it is. This philosophy is not widely accepted among U.S. librarians, but we need to take a closer look at this approach to determine its effectiveness.

RETRO ACCULTURATION

When both parents of Latino heritage become U.S. citizens, or when they have been born in the United States, it is likely that their children will be bilingual. As the second generation or third generation produces offspring, they will likely experience the phenomenon of retro acculturation. Retro acculturation is the act of becoming more familiar with one's history and culture. This will prolong the usage of Spanish. This usually manifests itself when second- and third-generation Latinos reflect on their culture by attending more cultural events, speaking Spanish, or enrolling their children in Spanish classes, to name a few examples.

What will the future of library services to Spanish-speakers look like? What are some of the issues that libraries will need to address today and in the future? How are they the same and how are they different? Currently, 25 percent of the Latino population is second generation. That number will grow significantly in the next 25 years; therefore, retro acculturation will be a more significant trait of second-generation households. Second-generation individuals know that being Latino is "okay," as they and their heritage are surfacing in a more positive manner in society than was the case for their parents.

FUTURE

As mentioned earlier in this *Crash Course* volume, something that you can always predict about the Spanish-speaking community is that they will be unpredictable. What we do know is that the population will continue to grow, whether it be first, second, or third generation. Within a few years, you are going to need to shift much of your efforts from a first-generation orientation to a second-generation point of reference. The Latino community in general is going to be much more politically involved and will be speaking and/or preferring English and code switching. They will be associating themselves with prominent and successful people as they compete for a large number of employment opportunities. They will want to be known for their character and professionalism, instead of being thought of only as someone from an under-represented group. Our approach needs to be overhauled to reflect the needs of second-generation Latinos.

CHAPTER 14

Conclusions

Despite the library's increasing involvement in community issues, Spanish-speakers often remain woefully uninformed about the many great resources in their communities, especially library services. In order for libraries to be considered serious social services providers within the community, we need to evaluate our approaches and philosophy.

This *Crash Course in Serving Spanish-Speakers* has put forward proven practices to assist you in entering this marketplace. Like any new library initiative where the outcome is unknown, you will need to learn to duck and weave from criticism and optimism. What we don't want to see is an unwieldy, inequitable, and undefined service agenda for Spanish-speakers. You and all librarians need to pursue this segment of the population in a well-thought-out, meticulous, and strategic manner. At the same time it must be highly tailored and culturally relevant. Most of these changes are predicated by several "R" words:

> **Reset.** Push the little button in your brain that will allow you to see Spanish-speaking people from a fresh new perspective. Avoid stereotypes and misinformation.

Reveal. Introduce and encourage the use of library services from the cultural perspective of Spanish-speakers by revealing the library's many great resources in a way with which they can connect.

Respect. See Spanish-speakers in the foreground rather than the background. Consider them as you would consider any respectable people.

Relate. Find out what is Latino in your library and start from there. Don't jump too far ahead of people or you will lose them.

Repeat. Repeat what you have to offer and how people can benefit from your services, over and over again, because Spanish-speaker are often not familiar with library services. Address one aspect of your Spanish services for four to six months and then gradually move to another aspect for the same period of time.

Reframe. Approach from angle of what others have to gain from your services instead of what you have to offer. If they don't need it, they won't use it. If there is something in it for them, they will capitalize on it.

I hope that this crash course has served as an invaluable resource for informing, challenging, and inspiring library systems and librarians. As a dynamic segment of the community, the Spanish-speakers of today will change with every generation. This will mean that current library approaches must also be dynamic. It is our intention that the ideas presented here are fresh and timely, as more parts of the United States are going to see more Spanish-speakers. By following the mentioned approaches, you will turn intentions or goals into results. These results will empower Spanish-speaking communities, educate Spanish-speakers, and forge a successful future for all. Let's push one step beyond the simplistic approach into what is truly an empirical approach. It might be an option now, but it will be a necessity in the near future. Providing successful library services to Spanish-speakers starts right here and right now.

¡Buena Suerte!

APPENDIX A

List of Magazines

Automundo
Buenhogar
Casa & Estilo Internacional
Casa de las Améritas
Cosmopolitan en Español
Cristina: La Revista
Discover en Español
Estylo
Fama
Furia Musical
Gatopardo
Glamour en Español
Hola
Ideas para su Hogar
Iguana
Imagen
Impacto Latino
Men's Health—Spanish Edition
Mira!

National Geographic en Español
Newsweek en Español
People en Español
Popular Mechanics en Español
Prevention en Español
Rolling Stone, Spanish edition
Selecciones del Reader's Digest
Siempre
Telva
Think Spanish
Tu
Tu Bebe
TV y Novelas
Vamos
Vanidades Continental
Vida Cristiana y Carisma
Vogue España
Zoobooks, Spanish edition

APPENDIX B

East Las Vegas
Library Service Plan

The East Las Vegas Library Service Plan is divided into five parts: Community Analysis, Programs and Services, Collections, Outreach, and Staffing. The Service Plan assists staff in implementing library services that are relevant to the community. In addition, it serves as a guide for staff to offering a unique service program that includes new methods for reaching and serving the community, ensuring that the library provides services that are responsive and enhance the quality of life of the residents it serves.

SECTION I: COMMUNITY ANALYSIS

The East Las Vegas Library is located on Lamb Boulevard in the William K. Moore Elementary School and was developed cooperatively with the Clark County School District. The East Las Vegas Library serves areas bordered by Owens Avenue to the north, Nellis Boulevard to the east, Eastern Avenue to the west and Sahara Avenue to the south. This area is a high-density segment of the community that is

95

perceived, internally and externally, to be without access to library services. Current population for this area is estimated at 188,244 and is projected to increase to 197,091 by 2007. Approximately 13,000 elementary, middle, and high school students are served.

Population Characteristics

Census data reveals that this service area is predominantly of Latino heritage, is very young, has more than the average number of persons per household, has a lower educational attainment, speaks Spanish in half the households, and is of a relatively low socioeconomic status. Traditionally, members of this community are not familiar with library services, either because of educational or economic backgrounds. According to a February 23, 2003 *Las Vegas Sun* article titled "State Tries to Close a Spanish Gap," "Nevada now ranks sixth in the nation in the percentage of its population that speaks Spanish at home." Median age for the service area is 28, 40 percent of the population is under 20 years of age, and 19 percent or 4,986 people in the service area are aged 5 years and older.

Educational Organizations

There are nine elementary schools, three middle schools, and one high school in the service area. The student body population for the service area is 13,000. The District-wide Accountability Reports of the Clark County School District (CCSD) lists these schools as at-risk. As a result these schools offer special programs. The Accountability Reports indicate that these schools have a high percentage of students receiving free/reduced meals and a high percentage of students enrolled in English Language Learner (ELL) classes. These reports also show a lower percentage of proficient students and a moderate level of parental involvement. The Nevada Department of Education reported the high school dropout rate among Hispanics to be 7.9 percent. One third of Clark County School District dropouts are Hispanic. Given these factors, the East Las Vegas Library has the opportunity to play an important role in supporting educational programs and student achievement.

Community Organizations

Vital library services to the entire community are more successful when library activities are coordinated with community organizations, associations, community centers, adult education providers, churches, and social services providers. Local agencies that represent potential partners include neighborhood associations and leisure services facilities.

SECTION II: PROGRAMS AND SERVICES

Services in Branch

This branch offers traditional and nontraditional library services including circulating collections, reference assistance, general information assistance, and referrals to other community agencies. A primary focus of the branch is homework help, which is offered Monday to Friday from 3 to 5 PM. A central reference desk serves both the children's and adults' areas. A computer lab, homework center, story room, classroom, and public meeting space play key roles in the delivery of homework assistance, literacy, ESL, ELL, civics, and GED instruction. A mobile laptop computer lab supplements the computer lab. Instruction on how to use library resources to find information is offered regularly.

Programs in Branch

Weekly story times are offered with particular emphasis on family literacy and prereading skills. Programs for preschool children include sharing books, flannel boards, poems, and music. Videos are used to enhance programs.

After-school programming emphasizes homework help to students grades 3 through 12. Additionally, there are special programs for school-aged children from kindergarten through 12 grade, featuring books, crafts, and learning-to-read activities. Teen programs include a volunteering component, as well as featured guests, crafts, and activities.

Special programs for adults emphasize life skills such as job skills, resume writing, interview skills, parenting, how to start a business, tax preparation, and parenting skills. Special efforts are made to reach families and to encourage participation in family literacy programs.

The library serves as a forum for sharing community information and as a clearinghouse for cultural heritage programs to attract families. Partnerships are forged with city and county agencies to offer the following types of services: shot clinics, voters registration , business licensing, adult education, and vocational classes. These partnerships allow other community organizations and agencies to distribute information at the library as well as work with library staff to cosponsor programs.

The library's facilities make it possible for organizations and businesses to meet with members of the community to disseminate information on services available to the community.

SECTION III: OUTREACH

Outreach efforts by the staff of the East Las Vegas Library are one of the most important factors in ensuring that the library is meeting the needs of the community.

In particular, the Branch Outreach Librarian is responsible for rendering this unique service as part of the outreach initiatives. Outreach efforts focus on community visits, community programs, and establishing partnerships within the service area. Targeted populations in the service area include families, Latinos, children, seniors, and teens.

Community Visits

Community visits focus on schools, day care centers, community centers, and other organizations in the community where small groups of community members are gathered and need to be introduced to library services. Visits supply information about materials, computer services, and upcoming programming events, as well as specific information geared to meeting a specific community need. The Branch Outreach Librarian is responsible for outreach efforts. In addition, s/he coordinates branch outreach efforts.

The Children's Services staff focus their community visits on elementary and middle schools, day care centers, safe key programs, and other community organizations catering to children. Adult Services staff focus their community visits on high schools, community centers, and other community organizations catering to adults and teens.

Community Programs

Community Programs focus on disseminating information to community members through large organized events such as school fairs, community centers' events, swap meets, and participation with local businesses. Outreach done at community programs include staffing booths to hand out the latest library information on programs and services as well as an opportunity to meet and help community members with their informational needs on a one-on-one basis. Staff also participate heavily in district-wide outreach events such as back-to-school fairs at local malls and cultural celebrations at community parks.

Outreach Targets

Elementary Schools

William K. Moore Elementary School

Oran K. Gragson Elementary School

Robert Lunt Elementary School

William E. Snyder Elementary School

Walter Bracken Elementary School

C.C. Ronnow Elementary School

Arturo Cambeiro Elementary School

Middle & High Schools

Roy W. Martin Middle School

John C. Fremont Middle School

K.O. Knudson Middle School

Desert Pines High School

Sunrise Acres Elementary School

Walter V. Long Elementary School

Day Cares

A1 Baby Sitting Services

Angel Care Child Care

Back to Basic Preschool

Children's Oasis

Childtime Children's Center (3)

Creative Beginnings (2)

First Step Kids Care

Geneva Boley Family Home

Grandma's Day Care

Kids Cove Daycare & Preschool

Kinder Care Learning Center

La Petite Academy

Lit'l Scholar Academy

Maria Amazcua Family Home

Montessori School of Las Vegas

Playtime Child Care

Rhonda L. Cox Family Care Home

Theresa Baca Family Care Home

Theresa FAU Family Care Home

Tinker Town Learn & Play Center

Trinity Life Pre-school

Churches

PRIMARY (WITHIN 1 MILE)

Jesus Lamb of God

Lamb Blvd. Missionary Baptist

Mountain View Assembly of God

River of Life Fellowship

SECONDARY (WITHIN 89110 ZIP CODE)

Alpha & Omega Church

Blood of the Lamb Ministries

Church of Jesus Christ of LDS (2)

East Las Vegas Christian Center

Full Gospel Las Vegas Korean

Harbor Christian Fellowship

Jesus Lamb of God

Lamb Blvd. Missionary Baptist

Last Call Christian Fellowship

Mountain View Assembly of God

Orchard Baptist Church

St. Thomas Episcopal Church

Sunrise Congregation-Jehovah's

Community and Government Organizations

Latin Chamber of Commerce

Clark County Family & Youth Services

Mexican Consulate

Clark County Parks & Community Services

Nevada Legal Services

Clark County Social Services

Nevada Business Services

City of Las Vegas Leisure Services

Nevada Division of Child & Family Service

City of Las Vegas Neighborhood Services

SECTION IV: COLLECTIONS

The East Las Vegas Library offers materials that have maximum use and circulation by ensuring that the branch collection reflects the interests and needs of the community. Areas of emphasis include Spanish-language material, literacy, youth collections, and homework help. Fifty percent of the collection targets youth. The collection comprises 60,000 volumes. Low shelving will be in place.

This branch is a model for the library district in its arrangement of collections to maximize the ability to browse and find materials with minimum use of the online catalog. Strategically placed bilingual signage supports browsing. In addition, teen and adult collections are featured with appropriate signage and the children's collection has low shelving.

Reading materials: Youth materials focus on getting ready to read, learning to read, and reading to learn in support of the Clark County School District's goal to have every child reading at grade level by the third grade.

Spanish language materials: The East Las Vegas Library has a large demand for materials in Spanish and bilingual texts. High-demand topics include literature, poetry, health, parenting, nutrition, pregnancy, cooking, motivation, the metaphysical, and biographies of popular entertainers and political figures. Youth materials in high demand include picture books, books for beginning readers, and nonfiction.

Literacy: Significant and appropriate materials to support ELL classes are critical. Four of the neighborhood elementary and middle schools currently offer ESL classes to parents. Computer Assisted Literacy in Libraries (CALL) programs for adults and families are active as well, coupled with civics, adult education, and GED preparation.

Youth and homework help: All service area schools offer extensive after-school tutoring and recreation programs. To support those community efforts, the library's youth collection emphasizes resources in reading, math, and science. The Young People's Library Department emphasizes collections that support learning to read (grades K-3 specifically). Based on popular after-school programs, recreational subjects for youth include learning to play musical instruments, chess, folk dance, and sports skills such as track and field, soccer, and boxing.

Popular materials in print and audio/visual (AV): Popular materials include bestsellers in Spanish and in English; movies in Spanish and those dubbed in Spanish; music; audio books; and nonfiction in video format on such topics as citizenship.

The collection also includes large numbers of uncataloged popular materials such as *fotonovelas* and other popular paperbacks. Popular AV materials include videos, DVDs and CDs.

Other collection areas of note: Periodicals include popular titles as *TV y Novelas*, *Vida Cristiana*, *Eres*, *Mecánica Popular*, and other titles that are likely to be found in a Latino establishment. Nonfiction subjects emphasize practical how-to information on becoming a citizen, living in the United States, jobs, health, housing, and education.

Reference: Extensive online resources supplement a core print reference collection. Professional resources such as "Criticas" and REFORMA help guide selections of popular and current materials in Spanish.

SECTION V: STAFFING

The East Las Vegas Library is open seven days, 72 hours a week. Service points covered include the circulation desk, reference/information desk, and computer lab. The reference/information desk serves the needs of all patrons and is staffed by both adult services and children's services staff.

Staff will consist of 10 full-time and 17 part-time positions for a total of 17.26 FTEs:

Full-Time Staff	**Part-Time Staff**
Branch Manager	YPL/Children's Assistant (2)
Young People's Library (YPL)/ Children's Department Head	Adult Services Assistant (2)
Adult Department Head	Circulation Assistant (5)
YPL/Children's Librarian	Computer Lab Assistant (3)
YPL/Children's Assistant	Pages (5)
Branch Outreach Librarian	
Adult Services Assistant	
Circulation Department Head	
Circulation Assistant	
Computer Lab Supervisor	

To provide flexibility in staff, either the YPL Children's Department Head position or the Adult Department Head position may serve as the Assistant Branch Manager. To meet the information needs of the community, all the staff that is assigned the role of Person in Charge (PIC) is bilingual in Spanish. In addition, the Circulation Department Head and the Computer Lab Supervisor are bilingual.

East Las Vegas Library
Service Plan
Staff Chart

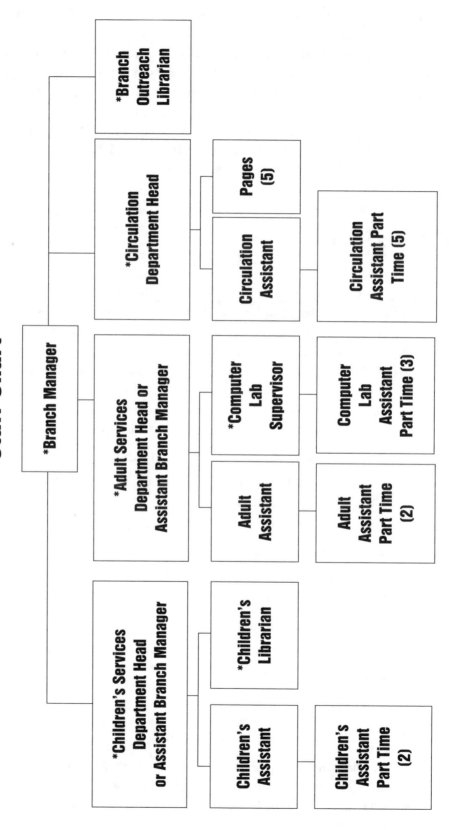

*Branch Manager

Children's Services Department Head or Assistant Branch Manager
- *Children's Librarian
- Children's Assistant
- Children's Assistant Part Time (2)

*Adult Services Department Head or Assistant Branch Manager
- *Computer Lab Supervisor
- Adult Assistant
- Computer Lab Assistant Part Time (3)
- Adult Assistant Part Time (2)

*Circulation Department Head
- Pages (5)
- Circulation Assistant
- Circulation Assistant Part Time (5)

*Branch Outreach Librarian

*Bilingual required (English and Spanish)

APPENDIX C

Internet Links

News

MSN Latinoamérica http://latam.msn.com/
Univision http://www.univision.com/
USA Latino http://usalatino.net/
CubaNet http://www.cubanet.org/
CNN en Español http://www.cnn.com/espanol/
MSN Latino http://latino.msn.com/
Periódicos Mexicanos en Linea http://periodicos.ws/

Immigration

Informacion sobre immigracion y visas
AILA http://www.aila.org/content/default.aspx?bc=9904
Inmigracion y visas http://www.inmigracionyvisas.com/index.html

Education

U.S. Department of Education http://www.ed.gov/espanol/
Aldea Educativa http://www.aldeaeducativa.com/

Parnaseo, Ciber-Paseo por la Literatura http://parnaseo.uv.es/
Political Database of the Americas http://pdba.georgetown.edu/
El Mundo.es Diccionarios http://www.elmundo.es/diccionarios/index.html?
    a=517c30d7e0b26770bf7e792978a9296e&t=1180649841
Diccionarios http://www.diccionarios.com/

Sports

ESPN Deportes http://espndeportes.espn.go.com/
Federación Mexicana de Fútbol Asociación http://www.femexfut.org.mx/portal
    v2/(wqmzizqtsubyiu2x5vd33355)/default.aspx

English as a Second Language

La Mansion del Ingles http://www.mansioningles.com/
English Spanish Link http://www.englishspanishlink.com/
Curso de Ingles Online http://www.curso-ingles.com/
Learn English http://www.lingolex.com/espan.htm

Health

Healthfinder http://www.healthfinder.gov/espanol/
U.S. Food and Drug Administration http://vm.cfsan.fda.gov/~mow/sinterna.html
Centers for Disease Control and Prevention http://www.cdc.gov/spanish/default.
    htm
Asegure a sus Hijos Ahora! http://www.insurekidsnow.gov/espanol/index.htm

Government

GovBenefits.gov http://www.govbenefits.gov/govbenefits_es.portal
Seguro Social en Español http://www.socialsecurity.gov/espanol/
Agency for Health Care Research and Quality http://www.ahcpr.gov/consumer/
    espanoix.htm
El Internet: Una Guía Para Padres de Familia http://www.ed.gov/pubs/parents/
    El_Internet/index.html
Federal Emergency Management Agency http://www.fema.gov/spanish/index_
    spa.shtm
Instituto Mexicano del Seguro Social http://www.imss.gob.mx/imss
U.S. Securities and Exchange Commission—*Informacion para los Inversionistas*
    http://www.sec.gov/investor/espanol.shtml
U.S. Consumer Product Safety Commission http://www.cpsc.gov/cpscpub/spanish/
    spanish.html
Acceso a todo el gobierno mexicano en la red http://www.directorio.gob.mx/
The White House http://www.whitehouse.gov/espanol/index.es.html
Seguro Social—Immigration http://www.ssa.gov/espanol/inmigracion/

Internal Revenue Service http://www.irs.ustreas.gov/espanol/index.html

U.S. Constitution (*Constitucion de los Estados Unidos de America*) http://pdba.
georgetown.edu/Constitutions/USA/usa1787.html

Alerta en Línea http://alertaenlinea.gov

Business

Banco de Desarrollo de América del Norte http://www.nadbank.org/espanol/
bdan.html

Entertainment

Quepasa http://www.quepasa.com/

La Raza Online http://www.laraza.com/

Vista Magazine http://www.vistamagazine.com/

Yahoo! Telemundo http://telemundo.yahoo.com/

Mundo Latino http://www.mundolatino.org/us.htm

Mundo Latino—El Rinconcito http://www.mundolatino.org/rinconcito/profesor.
htm

Colorín Colorado http://www.colorincolorado.org/

Latin Mail http://www.latinmail.com/

Lamira http://lamira.com

Computer

Internet de Mexico http://www.internet.com.mx/

Learn the Net/*Aprende el Internet* http://www.learnthenet.com/spanish/index.
html

Mexico Web http://www.mexicoweb.com.mx/

Yahoo! Mexico http://mx.yahoo.com/

Publicaciones Digitales http://biblioweb.dgsca.unam.mx/

SuperPages en Español http://espanol.superpages.com/

Google en Español http://www.google.com/intl/es/

Miscelleaneous

Instituto de Investigaciones Jurídicas de la Universidad Nacional Autonoma de
Mexico http://www.juridicas.unam.mx/

Organizacion de las Naciones Unidas (Onu) http://www.un.org/spanish/index.
shtml

Toda la Ley http://www.todalaley.com/

The Democratic Party http://www.democrats.org/espanol.html

Republic National Committee/*Comite Nacional Republicano* http://espanol.gop.
com/ Banco Interamericano de Desarollo

Bancomext http://www.bancomext.com/Bancomext/index.jsp

La Comicion Economica Para America Latina y el Caribe http://www.eclac.cl/

Consumers Union: *Documentos en Español* http://www.consumersunion.org/i/
     Spanish_Documents_-_En_Espanol/

Grupo del Banco Mundial http://www.bancomundial.org/

Invertia http://www.invertia.com/

Mujeres de Empresa: Negocios y capacitacion para la mujer emprendedora
     http://www.mujeresdeempresa.com/

Elmundolibro.com http://elmundolibro.elmundo.es/elmundolibro/

Libroadicto.com http://www.libroadicto.com/

These are only an introduction to the information that could be placed on your Web site. As you receive comments on what you have placed there, you will be able to make adjustments that will improve your Web site and make it more usable to Spanish-speakers.

APPENDIX D

Library of Congress Subject Headings (Translated)

A	General Works	Trabajos Generales
AC	Collections	Colecciones
AE	Encyclopedias	Enciclopedias
AG	General Reference Works	Trabajos Generales de Referencia
AI	Indexes	Índices
AM	Museums	Museos
AN	Newspapers	Periódicos
AP	Periodicals	Revistas
AY	Yearbooks	Anuarios
AZ	General History of Knowledge	Historia General del conocimiento
B	Philosophy & Religion	Filosofía y Religión
B	Collections	Colecciones
BC	Logic	Lógica
BD	Metaphysics	Metafísica
BF	Psychology	Psicología
BH	Esthetics	Estética
BJ	Ethics	Ética
BL	Religión & Mythology	Religión y mitología

BM	Judaism	Judaísmo
BP	Islam	Islam
BQ	Buddhism	Budismo
BR	Christianity	Cristiandad
BS	Bible & Exegesis	Biblia y exégesis
BT	Doctrinal Theology	Teología doctrinal
BV	Practical Theology	Teología práctica
BX	Denominations	Denominaciónes
C	History—Auxiliary Sciences	Historia—Ciencias auxiliaries
CB	History of Civilization	Historia de la Civilización
CC	Archaeology	Arqueología
CD	Archives & Diplomatics	Archivos y Diplomados
CE	Technical Chronology	Cronología Técnica
CJ	Numismatics	Numismática
CR	Heraldry	Heráldica
CS	Genealogy	Genealogía
CT	Biography	Biografía
D	History & Topography	Historia y Topografía
D	History (General)	Historia (General)
DA	Great Britain	Gran Bretaña
DB	Austria & Hungary	Austria y Hungría
DC	France	Francia
DD	Germany	Alemania
DE	Mediterranean Region	Región Mediterranea
DF	Greece	Grecia
DG	Italy	Italia
DH-DJ	Netherlands & Belgium	Holanda y Bélgica
DK	Russia	Rusia
DL	Scandinavia	Escandinavia
DP	Spain & Portugal	España y Portugal
DQ	Switzerland	Suiza
DR	Turkey & Europe	Turquía y Europa
DS	Asia	Asia
DT	Africa	Africa
DU	Australia	Australia
DX	Gypsies	Gitanos
E	U.S. History	Historia de los Estados Unidos
F	United States & Americas	Estados Unidos (local) y América
G	Geography—Anthropology	Geografía y antrolopía
G	Geography	Geografía general
GA	Geography & Cartography	Geografía y cartografía
GB	Physical Geography	Geografía física

GC	Oceanography	Oceanografía
GF	Anthropogeography	Antropogeografía
GN	Anthropology & Ethnology	Antropología y Etnología
GR	Folklore	Folklore
GT	Manners & Customs	Costumbres y tradiciones
GV	Sports & Games	Deportes y juegos
H	Social Sciences	Ciencias Sociales
H	Social Sciences (General)	Ciencias Sociales en general
HA	Statistics	Estadísticas
HB	Economic Theory	Teoría Económica
HC	Economic History	Historia de la Economía
HD	Land, Agricultura & Real Estate	Tierra, Agricultura e inmuebles
HE	Transporation & Communication	Transportación y comunicación
HF	Commerce, Business & Computer	Comercio, negocio y computadoras
HG	Finance	Finanzas
HJ	Public Finance	Finanzas Públicas
HM	Sociology	Sociología
HN	Social History & Problems	Historia social y problemas
HQ	Family, Marriage & Sexuality	Familia, matrimonio y sexualidad
HS	Societies	Sociedades
HT	Communities, Classes & Races	Comunidades, razas y clases
HV	Social Pathology, Welfare	Patología social, bienestar
HX	Socialism, Communism	Socialismo, Comunismo
J	Political Sciences	Ciencias políticas
J	Official Documents	Documentos oficiales
JA	General Works	Trabajos Generales
JC	Political Sciences: Theory of State	Ciencia política: teoría del estado
JF	Constitutional History	Historia constitucional
JK	United States & Citizenship	Estados Unidos y ciudadanía
JL	British America & Latin America	America Británica y America Latina
JN	Europe	Europa
JQ	Asia, Africa & Australia	Asia, Africa y Australia
JS	Local Government	Gobierno local
JX	International Law	Leyes Internacional
K	Law	Ley
KF 297–334	Legal Profession	Profesión legal
KF 501–553	Family Law	Leyes Familiares
KF 746–780	Wills & Estates	Testamentos y estados
KF 1501–1548	Bankruptcy	Bancarrota
KF 1600–2940	Commercial Law	Leyes Comerciales
KF 4501–5130	Constitution	Constitución
KF 8700–9075	Criminal Law	Leyes Criminales
L	Education & General Works	Educación y trabajos generales

LA	History	Historia
LB	Theory & Practice	Teoría y práctica
LB 1050	Reading & Primary Education	Lectura y educación primaria
LB 2350	College Entrance & Financing	Entrada al colegio y finanzas
LB 2369	Term Papers	Papeles de terminación
M	Music	Música
M 5–1459	Instrumental Music	Música instrumental
M1495–1998	Vocal Music	Música vocal
M1999–2199	Secular	Secular
ML	Literatura of Music	Literatura músical
MT	Music Instruction & Study	Enseñanza y estudio de la música
N	Fine Arts & Visual Arts	Artes finas y visuales
NA	Architecture & Computer Design	Arqictectura y diseño por computadora
NB	Sculpture	Escultura
NC	Drawing, Design & Illustration	Dibujo, diseño e ilustraciones
ND	Painting	Pintura
NE	Print Media	Medios de impresión
NK	Decorative & Applied Arts	Decoración y artes aplicadas
NX	Arts in General	Arte en general
P	Language & Literature	Lengua y literatura
P	Philology & Linguistics	Filología y lingüística
PA	Classical Languages & Literature	Literatura clásica y lenguas
PC	Romance Languages	Lenguas romance
PD	Germanic Languages	Lenguas germánicas
PE	English	Ingles
PF	West Germanic	Germánico oeste
PH	Finish & Hungarian	Filandés y Hungaro
PJ	Egyptian, Semitic Middle Eastern	Semítico y medio este eqipcio
PK	Indo-Iranian	Indoirani
PL	Languages & Literature of Asia	Lenguas y literature de Asia
PM	American Indian Languages	Lenguas Indias Americanas
PN	Literary History & Collection	Historia y colección literaria
PQ	Romance Literature	Literatura romance
PR	English Literature	Literatura Inglesa
PS	American Literature	Literatura Americana
PT	Germanic Literature	Literatura germánica
Q	Science	Ciencias
Q	Science (General)	Ciencias (general)
QA	Mathematics & Computer History	Matemáticas e historia de la computación
QB	Astronomy	Astronomía
QC	Physics	Física

QD	Chemistry	Química
QE	Geology	Geología
QH	Natural History	Historia natural
QL	Zoology	Zoología
QM	Human Anatomy	Anatomía Humana
QP	Physiology	Fisiología
QR	Microbiology	Microbiología
R	Medicine	Medicina
RA	Public Health	Salud pública
RB	Pathology	Patología
RC	Internal Medicine	Medicina interna
RD	Surgery	Cirugía
RF	Ear, Nose & Throat	Oído, nariz y garganta
RG	Gynecology	Ginecología
RJ	Pediatrics	Pediatría
RK	Dentistry	Odontología
RL	Dermatology	Dermatología
RM	Therapeutics & Diet Therapy	Terapéutica y terapia alimentocía
RS	Pharmacy	Farmacología
RT	Nursing	Enfermería
RX	Homeopathy	Homeopatía
RZ	Other systems of medicine	Otros ciencias de la medicina
S	Agriculture Plant & Animal Industry	Agricultura de plantas e industria animal
S	Agriculture (General)	Agricultura en general
SB	Plant Culture	Cultivo de plantas
SB 318–450	Horticulture	Horticultura
SB 469–479	Landscape Gardening	Paisaje de jardinería
SB 599–1100	Pest & Diseases	Peste y enfermedades
SD	Forestry	Ingeniería forestal
SF	Animal Culture	Cria de animales
SF 411–459	Pets	Mascotas
SF 461–513	Birds	Pájaros
SH	Aquaculture & Fishing	Pesca y aquacultura
SK	Hunting	Cacería
T	Technology & Drafting	Tecnología y dibujo mecánico
TA	Engineering (General)	Ingeniería general
TB	Hydraulic Engineering	Ingeniería hidráulica
TC	Environmental Technology	Tecnología ambiental
TD	Environmental Pollution	Contaminación ambiental
TE	Highway Engineering	Ingeniería de carreteras
TF	Railroad Engineering	Ingeniería de ferrocarriles
TG	Bridge Engineering	Ingeniería de puentes

TH	Building Construction	Construcción de edificios
TJ	Mechanical Engineering	Ingeniería Mecánica
TK	Electrical Engineering	Ingeniería eléctrica
TL	Motor Vehicles	Vehículo motorizados
TN	Mining & Mineral Industries	Minería e Industria de minas
TP	Chemical Technology	tecnología química
TR	Photography	Fotografía
TS	Manufacturers	Manufactura
TT	Handicrafts	Manualidades o artesanias
TX	Home Economics	Economía domestica
TX 645–840	Cookbooks	Libros de cocina
TX 901–953	Hotel & Food Service	Hoteles y servicios de comida
U	Military Science	Ciencia militar
V	Naval Science	Ciencia Naval
Z	Bibliography & Library Science	Bibliografía y ciencias bibliotecarias
Z 4–8	History of Books	Historia de los Libros
Z 49–51	Typing	Mecanografía
Z 52	Word Processing	Procesamiento de textos
Z 53–102	Shorthand	taquigrafía
Z 662–1000	Libraries	Bibliotecas
Z 1001–8999	Bibliographies	Bibliografías

BIBLIOGRAPHY

Alvarez, Julia. 2007. *Once Upon a Quinceañera: Coming of Age in the USA*. New York: Viking.

Castillo, Franziska. 2006. "The Crisis Facing Our Boys." *Latina*, November, 92.

Collins, James C. 2005. *Good to Great and the Social Sector*. Boulder, Colo.: Jim Collins.

Gomez, Martin. 2000. "Who Is Most Qualified to Serve Our Ethnic-Minority Communities?" *American Libraries*, December, 39.

Gravenhorst, Edna C. 2007. *Ay, Mijo! Why Do You Want to Be an Engineer?* St. Louis, MO; E. C. Gravenhorst.

Hartman, Taylor. 1998. *The Color Code*. New York: Simon & Schuster.

Harvey, William C. 2000. *Outreach Spanish*. New York: Barrons.

Novinger, Tracy. 2001. *Intercultural Communication: A Practical Guide*. Austin, Tex.: University of Texas Press.

Perez-Brown, Maria. 2003. *Mamá: Latina Daughters Celebrate Their Mothers*. New York: Rayo.

Poniatowska, Elena. 2006. *Las Soldaderas: Women of the Mexican Revolution*. El Paso, Tex.: Cinco Punto Press.

Rodriguez, Richard. 2002. *Brown: The Last Discovery of America*. New York: Viking.

Sawyer, Chrysanthe G. 2007. "Marketing to Hispanics Requires a Culture-Specific Approach." *Business Press: Las Vegas*, January 1, 13.

Tradiciones Mexicanas. 2005. Mexico: Editorial Epoca.

Vasquez, Richard. 2005. *Chicano*. New York: Rayo.

INDEX

ABOUT THE AUTHOR

SALVADOR AVILA is a Branch Manager in the Las Vegas—Clark County Library District, in Las Vegas, Nevada.